Integrated

Design

in

Contemporary

Architecture

Integrated Design in

Contemporary Architecture

————

Kiel Moe

PRINCETON ARCHITECTURAL PRESS

NEW YORK

Published by
Princeton Architectural Press
37 East Seventh Street
New York, New York 10003

For a free catalog of books, call 1.800.722.6657.
Visit our web site at www.papress.com.

Editor: Lauren Nelson Packard
Designer: Arnoud Verhaeghe

Special thanks to: Nettie Aljian, Sara Bader, Dorothy Ball, Nicola
Bednarek, Janet Behning, Becca Casbon, Carina Cha, Penny
(Yuen Pik) Chu, Russell Fernandez, Pete Fitzpatrick, Wendy Fuller,
Jan Haux, Clare Jacobson, Aileen Kwun, Nancy Eklund Later,
Linda Lee, Laurie Manfra, Katharine Myers, Jennifer Thompson,
Paul Wagner, Joseph Weston, and Deb Wood of Princeton
Architectural Press —Kevin C. Lippert, publisher

Library of Congress Cataloging-in-Publication Data
Integrated design in contemporary architecture / Kiel Moe.—1st ed.
  p.   cm.
ISBN: 978-1-56898-745-3 (hardcover : alk. paper)
1. Sustainable architecture—United States. 2. Architecture—United
States—21st century.
NA2542.36.M64 2008
720—dc22
                                            2008005145

# Contents

# Preface

## Sustainability and Integrated Design

The concept of sustainability is an increasingly important issue for society, and it is becoming central to multiple aspects of public and private life. Unfortunately, the concept of "sustainable architecture" has been applied and marketed so freely that it is now a vague, if not unreliable, concept. More importantly, this term does not indicate anything about how an architect might learn and practice architecture differently in order to engage the complex factors and principles that lead toward more sustainable building practices *and* better design. "Integrated design" is a term that characterizes what architects and architecture students do when they incorporate the energy, site, and climatic, formal, construction, programmatic, regulatory, economic, and social aspects of a project as primary parameters for design. The result is often better building design and building performance on account of a fundamental engagement with these multiple, often complex, contexts that condition contemporary architecture. In doing so, practitioners engender what could be more sustainable modes of practice. If architecture becomes more sustainable, it is because its practices and buildings will have fundamentally become more integrated.

## Complexity, Composition, and Integrated Design

Contemporary architecture is characterized by a growing awareness of its inherent complexities. While the notion of complexity in architecture is occasionally expressed in complex building shapes, the actual complexity of architecture is difficult to apprehend visually. Rather than the composition of static objects, complexity in architecture can be more productively understood in terms of its own contingencies, performances, and potential effects. Any building project is contingent upon an idiosyncratic assemblage of theoretical, practical, ecological, economical, political, social, and cultural parameters that presuppose the design and performance of architecture. Reflexively, architecture in turn affects these parameters. The role of architecture in the effectuation of sustainability is a prime

example. The real complexity of architecture is in the cogent organization and integration of these multivariate parameters, directing its potential effects toward some larger end through an architectural agenda.

Integrated design is typified by architects integrating and practicing this complexity. Thus integrated design involves not only deftly integrating the increasing complexity of building production—an expanding list of consultants and communications, increasingly complex building technologies and envelopes, energy efficient techniques and technologies, software, fabrication and construction delivery methods, economic and ecological limits—but it also formally incorporates and directs the behavior of complexity. Complexity in scientific thinking focuses upon systems that self-organize or otherwise produce novel effects not evident in the initial conditions or state of a system. Familiar examples include practices that either denigrate a milieu (ecological, economic, or social) versus practices that sponsor mutually beneficial and productive ends for multiple, simultaneous milieus. The difference between the two practice types is the degree to which the respective agencies acknowledge and integrate the complexities of the assemblage that presupposes their work.

Depending upon the context, integrated design may mean that a building's spatial, construction, energy, and systems logics are intertwined. It may also mean that a building is the product of new social relationships amongst architects, clients, developers, builders, communities, and consultants. Integrated design inevitably means many things to different practices depending on the context, however, each form of integration promises new futures for architecture and its constituencies. In all cases, it is apparent that architects are uniquely positioned to engage the systemic nature of integrated practices that will characterize the new century. While architecture may not yet have overt theories of integration, all complexity thinking requires creativity, multiple variable problem-solving, spatial and temporal thinking, the ability to visualize complex phenomena, and the ability to articulate rich—if not simple—and appropriate solutions to complex information. These are all characteristics evident in architectural education and are certainly evident in the following projects and practices.

Another important theme from complexity thinking, in all the following projects, is that the concept of context is shifting to more comprehensive and productive applications that reflect the inherent complexity of architecture. No longer merely the adjacent real estate surrounding a project, each of the following projects emerges from a much more conscientious understanding of the systemic yet idiosyncratic contexts of any project: physical, social, economical, ecological, climatic, regulatory, and programmatic. Integrated design fundamentally involves a strategic reconstructing of the given, yet broadly defined, context(s) of a project.

The incorporation of architecture's complex contexts is central to integrated design and accordingly shifts what constitutes the term "composition" in architecture. Until recently, this term had always been dominated by the logic of a visual image. The logic of construction and its delivery, the logic of a high-performance building, or the logic of a particular market condition, for instance, provide equally potent and rigorous logics for composition alongside the role of visual logic. In the following buildings, it is clear that what composes *architecture* materially and immaterially is a broadened understanding of context and the multivariate assemblage of factors and forces that compose *buildings*. In the following buildings, this understanding of "composition" is particularly evident at the confluence of two salient aspects of this expanded understanding of context: the energy milieu of every building site and the social construction of architecture.

## Energy and Architecture

The premise of the following buildings is that energy, construction, and formal strategies should be inextricably interlocked. The morphology of each building's composition actively seeks to merge architectural intentions with constitutive parameters such as site, climate, energy consumption, materials, and construction. Each can be understood as a material device that captures and channels specific energy paths. As such, these projects clearly illustrate a key characteristic of integrated design that Reyner Banham discerned in his 1969 *The Architecture of the Well-tempered Environment* between "power-operated solutions" and "structural solutions." Power-operated solutions tend to add ever more energy and yet another layer of construction to solve each problem that arises in the context of building design. This approach characterizes building production in the second half of the twentieth century. During this period, buildings became hermetically sealed, relied upon an increasingly layered approach to construction, and used increasing amounts of energy to serve their occupants. This approach was once understandable given its, now-distant, context of seemingly endless and relatively cheap energy sources. However, this is not a viable strategy for architecture in our current professional, economical, social, and ecological context.

Alternatively, the structural solutions Banham distinguished inevitably merge energy and construction strategies with architectural intentions as key determinants of architectural form. They are structural solutions because the physical configuration of the building form and the fabric of the building itself induce certain energy performances. In short, the energy and construction solutions are structured simultaneously. As such, these buildings are thermodynamic figures. In this type of compositional figuration, the behavior of immaterial building thermodynamics directly influences a building's material morphology. These thermodynamic figures are best understood and designed in a building's section where the dynamics of light, air, and heat are most active. Some of the most compelling work in integrated design today occurs in thermodynamic figures that bear an anomalous convergence of the maximal within the minimal: each of the buildings in this book inevitably tend toward maximum performance with minimal means. The result is buildings that are shaped as much by building physics as by any other traditional morphological agent, such as the body, program, or style. If a seminal question of architectural form has been what gives a building its shape, that question remains in integrated design.

One certain outcome of integrated design is a drastic minimization of power-operated convection-based heating, ventilating, and air-conditioning (HVAC) systems. Given that contemporary HVAC systems may absorb a third or even half of a building's budget and an equal portion of its energy budget, the active architectural surfaces of a structural solution inherently redirects budget, material, labor, energy, design time, coordination, and maintenance away from conventional HVAC systems and toward the fabric of the building itself, imbuing it with a more active role. In most of the following projects, there is a compelling tendency to activate the embodied energy and composition of a structural solution as a key component of a building's energy performance. Aspects of integrated design collapse the layers of contemporary construction systems into more poignant, performative, and fewer layers of construction. Thermally active surfaces abound in these projects. The Gleneagles Community Center is a prime example of this trajectory. The ambitious modesty of the Lovejoy Building and the Pittsburgh Glass Center are also examples of this approach. The Glass Pavilion at the Toledo Museum of Art is a discrete example that strategically employs thermally active surfaces to enable its transparency in its climate.

In addition to the thermal activation of surfaces, the full activation of the building envelope is another common feature of these buildings. As opposed to the twentieth-century view of the building envelope as a static and hermetically sealed boundary, the building envelope in integrated design is a dynamic entity, an articulated device that selectively captures and channels various forms of energy between the interior and exterior. This is evident in several architectural strategies that capture energy, air, and water available on each building site and channel them to where they are most productive. The Lavin-Bernick Center for University Life at Tulane University is a prime example of this thinking. The intensely developed building envelopes in this book represent a catalog of techniques for managing the energy exchanges that occur in every building milieu. In their idiosyncratic ways, the New Residence at the Swiss Embassy, the North Carolina Museum of Art, the Sidwell Friends School, the Water + Life Museums, the Chicago Residence, and the Museum of Contemporary Art in Denver each use the building envelope to capture and channel the dynamic solar energy system of their site to activate the architecture and its energy systems. Similarly, an analysis conducted during the renovation of Mies van der Rohe's Crown Hall revealed that the operative boundary of the original building's energy strategy extended out to include the seasonal variations of Alfred Caldwell's original deciduous landscape plan. In the Fire Station 10 project, minimal energy strategies reinforce a fundamental program requirement of full operation for several days without utilities in the event of a disaster. As such, integrated design envisions a building as a capture-and-channel device that directs the energy flows in any building. In all cases, this results in architecture that is more productive and dynamic.

Many of these energy and construction strategies are often referred to as "passive" or "natural" techniques. These misnomers are unfortunate and misguiding because such strategies are clearly active physically, thermodynamically, and conceptually in the buildings included here. As the Milton Academy Science Building and the Seminar II Building at the Evergreen State College both demonstrate, Banham's notion of structural solutions is at once a more accurate and reliable description of the energy strategies and approaches employed in these buildings. It is precisely the activation of otherwise often-ignored material and energy systems that engenders the integrated aspects of each building. Likewise, there is recognition of the decidedly non-natural state of a building and a city that engenders a more reliable relationship to the actual milieu and ecologies of a project. The south-facing additions to the University of Arizona College of Architecture and Landscape Architecture integrate aspects of the building and its landscape for certain performance, emblematic, and didactic purposes. Successfully integrated projects appear to emphasize the ecologies of buildings and the building of ecologies less for their moralistic or rhetorical content, and more for their pragmatic content because ecology's concepts and vocabularies describe the dynamic spatial and temporal interactions of architecture in its physical milieu. Ecology focuses equally on the performances (properties and behaviors) and effects (social, aesthetic, ecological) of material-energy organizations such as landscapes, but increasingly at the urban and building scales as well. Similarly, the U.S. Border Patrol Station at Murrietta, California, integrates the physical and cultural landscape of the border region through its physical construction and its control of air and light. While these approaches to energy and construction are compelling, none are possible without a more overt recognition of the social construction of architecture.

## The Social Construction of Architecture

In integrated design, the distinction between power-operated solutions and structural solutions attains a new meaning beyond the energy strategies described above. In their own way, each of these projects shifts the power of authorship beyond the twentieth-century myth of the singular architect to thoroughly collaborative team structures that reflect the multivariate contexts of a project. As such, there is an acknowledgment in integrated design of the social construction of architecture that has not always been evident in recent periods of architecture. In this book, there is an explicit recognition that any building is a product of the social and technical contingencies that presuppose it. In each of these buildings, it is apparent that social integration precedes technical integration. All technology is social before it is technical. The complexities of building production inevitably require the expertise of multiple constituencies for viable and reliable solutions. Thus, the role of the architect has clearly shifted from individual master to strategic organizer of manifold, often disparate forms of knowledge and processes. This is most evident in the complex network of consultants and experts that presuppose and engender large projects, such as the Bank of America Tower at One Bryant Park and the Manitoba Hydro Downtown Office Project. Such projects inevitably have hundreds of individuals in dozens of areas of expertise that help structure and shape the production of these buildings. The emergence and incorporation of building physics consultants such as Transsolar, atelier ten, and Arup have rapidly advanced integrated building practices, as evident in numerous examples in this book. This recognition of architecture's social construction also fundamentally shifts the concept and activity of "composition" in architecture.

Certain software technologies are catching up to these social developments within the architecture, engineering, and construction industries. Building information modeling (BIM), for instance, promises to more intimately connect formerly disparate disciplines through streamlined communication and computation abilities. SHoP Architects' optimization of a masonry building envelope in Manhattan integrates a broad range of software and production processes to execute this new construction. Similarly, Morphosis uses BIM on projects such as the U.S. Federal Building in San Francisco to align its formal ambitions with economic, energy, and scheduling parameters.

In some cases, the technical aspects of integrated design overtly work to serve the social agendas of a project. The Lavin-Bernick Center for University Life at Tulane University uses its architecture and energy strategies to leverage programmatic and social situations not possible with a typical air-conditioned building in this climate. Similarly, the Interdisciplinary Science and Technology Building 2 creates a courtyard microclimate with its raw and frank construction systems to foster social interaction. In the 557/559 row houses, the energy and construction systems are the pretext of an urban housing marketing strategy that also aims to transform residential building practices as a pilot project. Another housing project, the Clarence, organizes a large housing development around a central courtyard, overlapping aspects of its energy strategies with public space response. In the case of the Artists for Humanity EpiCenter, a large array of photovoltaic panels powers the building. Likewise, the material and energy strategies of the Technology Access Foundation minimize initial and operational costs. This allows the institution to plan and direct their funding toward their social and artistic programs rather than operational energy costs.

A number of architecture schools now have active design-build programs that combine academic research and instruction-through-construction experience to build affordable housing in neighboring communities. Two compelling examples are included here. At the University of Virginia School of Architecture, the ecoMOD project has developed four houses that focus on the research, design, construction, and evaluation of energy-efficient prefabricated housing types. Each house is the product of cross-disciplinary seminars and design studios in which the economic and ecological performance of the housing is designed with equal rigor. Similarly, a new non-profit company directly associated with the College of Architecture and Landscape Architecture at the University of Arizona designs and implements affordable housing types in the Tucson empowerment zones in a unique delivery strategy that includes the labors of students, local developers, and builders. These academic programs no doubt point toward increasing levels of integrated design in the future as these architecture, engineering, planning, business, economics, and environmental science students mature into advanced professional roles throughout the building industry, based on these robust experiential learning experiences.

## Representation

One purpose of this book is to document the current representational strategies for integrated design that underlie each of the included integrated practices. The book presents a range of representational strategies and styles that attempt to visualize both the physical systems and the non-visual phenomena in an integrated design. However, certain representational strategies more accurately reflect the thermodynamic and luminous principles active in the performance of an integrated design. For example, a key distinction can be made between diagrammatic strategies that represent an energy flow as an arrow and those that represent energy as gradient fields. Arrows can be misleading. Although energy does flow, it always flows from a field of high intensity to a zone of lower intensity. The vector information is important to grasp, but the representation of the intensity fields presents a more complete view of the physical milieu of a project. Energy field intensities always exist in gradients and, thus, the most accurate representational strategies document these fields with some form of gradient information. This focus on the energy milieu, rather than just its flows, also prompts an architect to visualize the entire milieu as the basis of an integrated design, not just an isolated light or air flow. This helps identify other energy sources and sinks for a project. A sense of the total energy performance of a project from sun, wind, light, embodied energy, and life cycle analysis should be part of the energy strategy of a project from the start. An accurate—both intuitively and quantitatively—understanding of the physics involved in a building's physical milieu is essential to integrated design. The accuracy of early assumptions about energy and form will, and should, directly affect the morphology of a building design. An early and accurate understanding of these aspects are as important to integrated design as an operative understanding of structure, material costs, or program. The representational strategies also play an essential role in visualizing these critical non-visual phenomena to the non-expert constituencies that fund, operate, occupy, and maintain an integrated design.

## Conclusion

As canonical modernism—and even vestiges of the Beaux Arts—continues to recede as architecture moves into this new century, it is critical that architecture construct pedagogical and professional structures that position our students and professionals to expand their engagement with the integrated realities of practice in the new century. This is vital for the advancement of the economical, ecological, social, and formal basis of architecture, if not its mere perpetuation. Integrated design is at the core of this new vector in architecture. Architecture, however, has few, if any, theories of integration in its current discourse to direct such integrated design efforts. Nonetheless, the buildings included here provide ample built evidence of this type of thinking in practice. As in pragmatic thought, a theory of integration in architecture may be best discerned through experimentation and practice. Integration will be made, designed. Although European examples are often cited as models of integrated design, the intent of this book is to survey current approaches to integrated design practices applicable to North American code, climate, and economic contexts. This book provides twenty-eight examples of integrated design that cut across building types, budgets, climates, and locales. Regardless of budget or program, each project distills the increasing complexity of architecture's contingencies into coherent and integrated design.

# U.S. Federal Building

San Francisco, California

———

Morphosis, Santa Monica, California

**LEAD DESIGN ARCHITECT:** Morphosis
Thom Mayne, Principal; Tim Christ, Project Manager;
Brandon Welling, Project Architect; Project Team:
Linda Chung, Simon Demeuse, Marty Doscher,
Rolando Mendoza, Eui-Sung Yi; Project Assistants:
Caroline Barat, Gerald Bodziak, Crister Cantrell,
Delphine Clemenson, Todd Curley, Alasdair Dixon,
Haseb Faqirzada, Chris Fenton, Arthur de Ganay,
Dwoyne Keith, Sohith Perera, Kristine Solberg,
Natalia Traverso
**EXECUTIVE ARCHITECT:** Smith|Group: Carl Christiansen,
Project Manager; Jon Gherga, Project Architect;
Belinda Wong, Project Assistant
**COLLABORATIVE ARTISTS:** James Turrell, Ed Ruscha,
Rupert Garcia, Hung Liu, Raymond Saunders,
William Wiley
**STRUCTURAL, MECHANICAL, ELECTRICAL, AND PLUMBING
ENGINEER:** Arup; Steve Carter, Project Manager
**STRUCTURAL ENGINEERS:** Bruce Gibbons, Steve Ratchye
**MECHANICAL ENGINEER:** Erin McConahey
**NATURAL VENTILATION MODELING:** Lawrence Berkeley
National Laboratory
**LANDSCAPE ARCHITECT:** Richard Haag Associates with JJR
**CIVIL ENGINEER:** Brian Kangas Foulk
**GEOTECHNICAL ENGINEER:** Geomatrix
**LIGHTING CONSULTANT:** Horton Lees Brogden Lighting
Design
**SIGNAGE:** Kate Keating Associates
**COST ESTIMATOR:** Davis Langdon
**CURTAIN WALL:** Curtain Wall Design and Consulting
**BLAST CONSULTANT:** Hinman Consulting Engineers
**CODE CONSULTANT:** Rolf Jensen & Associates
**ACOUSTICS:** Thorburn Associates
**VERTICAL TRANSPORTATION:** Hesselberg, Keessee &
Associates
**CONSTRUCTION MANAGER:** Hunt Construction Group
**GENERAL CONTRACTOR:** Dick Corporation, Morganti
General Contractors

The 605,000 square-foot U.S. Federal Building in San Francisco activates its envelope and the fabric of the building to radically lower its energy consumption, lower its construction cost, and improve human comfort and productivity. Each of these ambitions informs and amplifies the formal goals of the project. Thus the project is determined neither by isolated formal preoccupations nor technical determinisms. Rather, this project productively merges both agendas through its integrated approach.

A crumpled metal skin clads the south side of the building. The perforated metal modulates solar loads while appearing nearly transparent from the interior, and engenders cross-ventilation strategies. The density of perforations blocks a controlled amount of light while simultaneously permitting views. The north side of the tower consists of vertically oriented solar control panels of laminated translucent glass. The vertical orientation is an appropriate strategy for the early morning and late afternoon solar loads for the orientation of this building surface. The translucent glass diffuses light and produces a compelling field surface treatment.

The dimensions and configuration of the floor plan are driven by daylighting and ventilation concerns. The narrow floor plates of the upper levels of the building (levels 5 through 18) have operable vents and windows that allow occupants to temper their environment. In the evenings, the building management system opens low supply-side vents for a night purging system. In this system, cool night air is drawn across the thermal mass of the ceiling, exchanging and evacuating heat energy from people and equipment loads that accumulated there during the day. The air is then exhausted through high exhaust-side vents. The building is cool by the following morning when employees arrive. The exposed concrete ceiling is profiled specifically to capture and pool heat in order to maximize the exchange

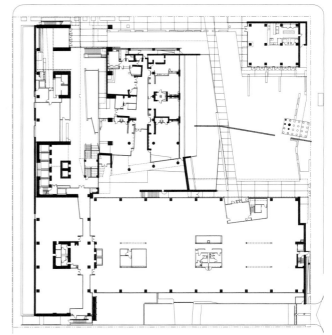

Ground floor plan

OPPOSITE
South facade

of heat with the night ventilation. To further facilitate this ventilation strategy, open office spaces line the perimeter of the floor plates with low-ceilinged offices and meeting rooms zoned in the middle of the floor plate. The tower uses a raised-floor system to distribute services. As evident here, the integration of services in the office tower typology has shifted from core-and-ceiling intensive to more intense floor and envelope strategies of the past several decades. Together, the desired dimensions for daylighting strategies, viable ventilation strategies, and building structure dimensions integrate well for office typologies.

The office portion of the building utilizes a skip-stop elevator strategy with elevator stops at every third floor to prompt more use of stairs as well as to minimize elevator loads and induce more employee exercise and interaction.

The morphology of this building composition and its construction is guided by specific integrated design strategies. Its construction, construction delivery, energy performance, and architectural performance were overtly integrated into its design process. This approach to integration is facilitated by building information modeling (BIM) that allows architects, contractors, and fabricators

to determine and control cost, engage alternative fabrication methods, accelerate construction, test energy and environmental strategies, and reduce errors and omissions. Although integrated on technical and physical levels, this software-centered approach also preserves more integrated social structures in the design process where various models are shared amongst designers, consultants, builders, and fabricators. Taken together, design approaches and decisions result in type-A office space with lower budgets, lower energy consumption, and with increased human comfort.

TOP LEFT: Lateral building section
BOTTOM LEFT: Skip-stop lobby
RIGHT: Skip-stop section

OPPOSITE
LEFT: Typical office plan
TOP RIGHT: Program organization
BOTTOM RIGHT: Circulation

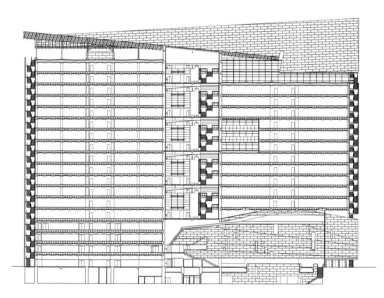

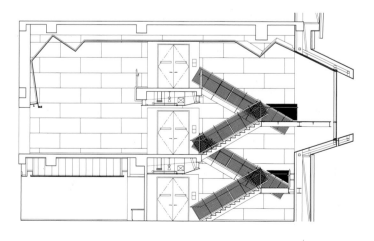

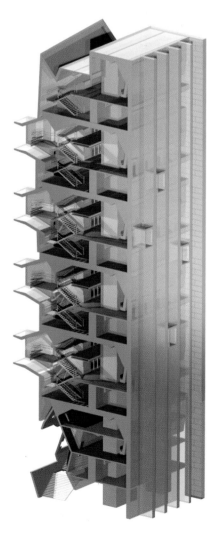

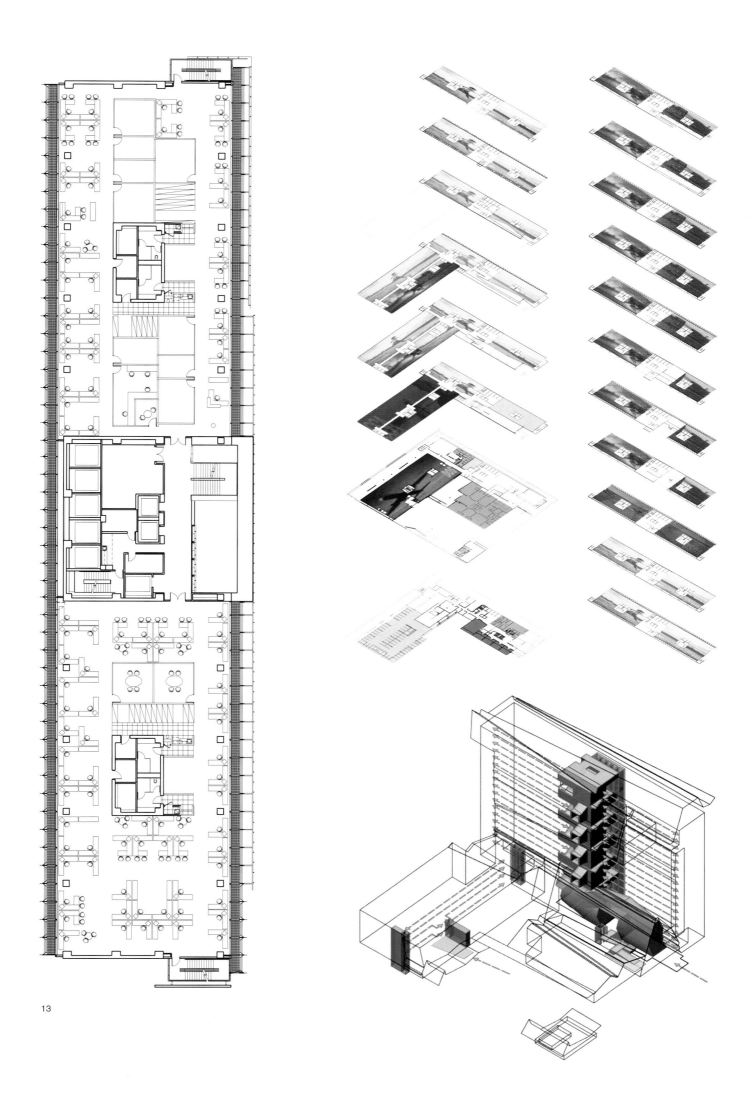

13

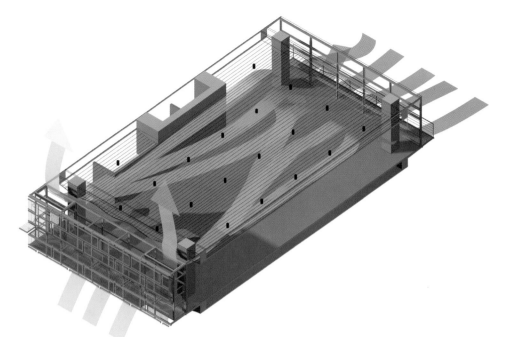

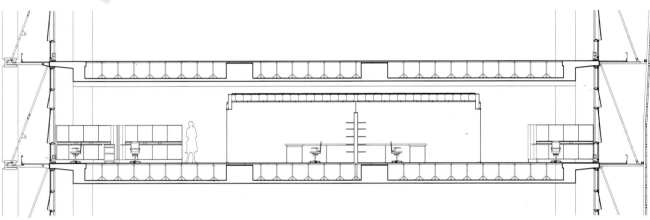

14

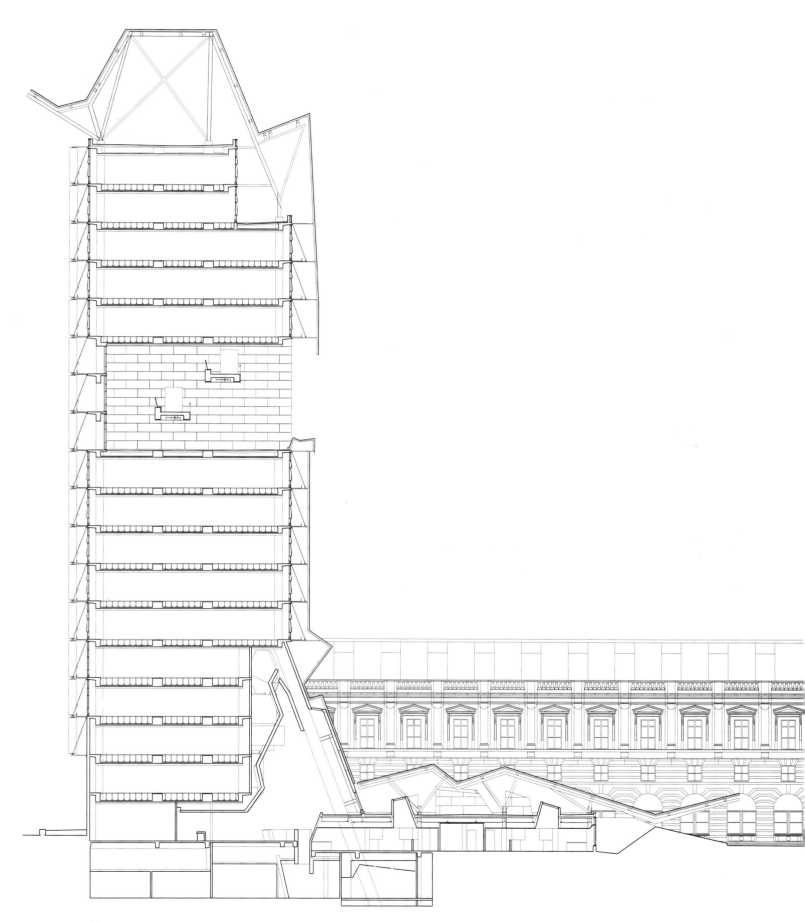

15

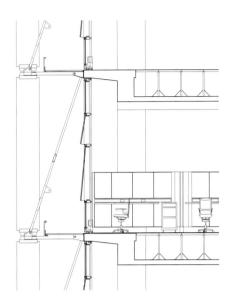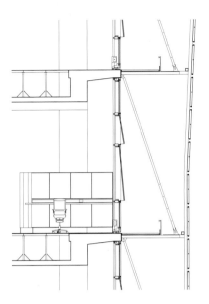

TOP: Building envelope
sections
BOTTOM: North facade

OPPOSITE
Solar control on north facade

# Manitoba Hydro Downtown Office Project

Winnipeg, Manitoba

Kuwabara Payne McKenna Blumberg Architects, Toronto, Ontario, with Smith Carter Architects and Engineers, Winnipeg, Manitoba, and Transsolar Energietechnik GmbH, Stuttgart

**MANITOBA HYDRO TEAM:** Tom Gouldsborough, Doug McKay, Kevin Leung, Colleen Johnson, Tom Akerstream, Julie Gervino, Leah Rensfelt, Susan Aird, Darren Sachvie, Carmen Hebert, Roberta Radons

**DESIGN ARCHITECT:** Kuwabara Payne McKenna Blumberg Architects

**IDP DESIGN CHARETTE TEAM:** Bruce Kuwabara, Luigi LaRocca, John Peterson, Javier Uribe, Taymoore Balbaa, Steven Casey, Andrew Dyke, Chu Dongzh, Omar Gandhi, Eric Ho, Steven Kopp, Norm Li, Francesco Valente-Gorjup

**DESIGN AND DOCUMENTS:** Bruce Kuwabara, Luigi LaRocca, John Peterson, Kael Opie, Lucy Timbers, Glenn MacMullin, Ramon Janer, Javier Uribe, Taymoore Balbaa, Clementine Chang, Virginia Dos Reis, Bettina Herz, Eric Ho, Tanya Keigan, John Lee, Norm Li, Eric Johnson, Andrea Macaroun, Rob Micacchi, Lauren Poon, Matt Storus, Richard Unterthiner, Dustin Valen, Marnie Williams, William Wilmotte, Paulo Zasso

**ARCHITECTS OF RECORD:** Smith Carter Architects and Engineers: Jim Yamashita, Partner in Charge; Rick Linley, Project Director; Glen Klym, Project Manager; Al Coppinger, John Crocker, Colin Reed, Ron Pidwerbesky, Architects; Kirk McLean, Project Coordinator; Matt Baker, Neil Hulme, Intern Architects; Phil Harmes, Stephane Chappellaz, Richard Chan, Dallas Ptosnick, Architectural Technologists; Brad Cove, Stephen Londrey, Specification Writers; Ron Martin, Senior Contract Administrator; Daryl Hnylycia, Contract Administrator; Sheila Reenders, Interior Designer; Lynne Richardson, Administrative

**ENERGY/CLIMATE ENGINEERS:** Transsolar: Thomas Auer, Alex Knirsch, Helmut Meyer, Nicole Kuhnert

**ADVOCATE ARCHITECT:** Prairie Architects: Dudley Thompson, Crystal Bornais, Teresa da Costa Neubauer, Dennis Kwan

**STRUCTURAL ENGINEER:** Crosier Kilgour & Partners Ltd.: Tom Malkiewicz, Joel Smith, John Wells, John Miller

**STRUCTURAL ENGINEER:** Halcrow Yolles: Barry Charnish, Project Executive; David Gray, Project Principal; Albert Mikhail, Project Engineer; Saeid Safadel, Design Engineer; Bushra Abolezz, Dorothy Pawluk, CAD drafters

**MECHANICAL AND ELECTRICAL ENGINEER:** Earth Tech Canada (ET Winnipeg) Alan Aftanas, Mike Burns, Jeff Brooks, Pertti Laitinen, Peter Tataryn, Steven Sadler, Daren Landers, Danvir Jhinger, David Perez, Sam Honcharik

**MECHANICAL ENGINEER (CALGARY):** John Munroe, Chris Saunders, Steve Ruel, Russell Bock, Herb Haekel, Jana Watson, Pak Chan, Brian Lockhart, Chris Himsl, David Michie, Lia LaClaire, Jay Campo

**ELECTRICAL ENGINEER (EDMONTON):** Mike Shewchuk, Selene Akano, Wally Alberda, Corey Weir

**LANDSCAPE ARCHITECT:** Hilderman Thomas Frank Cram: Garry Hilderman, Glen Manning; Phillips Farevaag Smallenberg: Greg Smallenberg, Jeff Staates

**GEOTHERMAL:** Groundsolar Energy Technologies, (Salmon Arm, B.C.) Jeff Quibell, Adam James; Omicron Consulting Group, Vancouver: Geoff McDonell

**LIGHTING:** Pivotal Lighting Design: Jeff Miller, Blythe von Reckers

**ACOUSTICS, AERCOUSTICS:** John O'Keefe, Emanuel Mouratidis

**VERTICAL TRANSPORTATION:** Soberman Engineering: Jon Soberman

**GEOTECHNICAL ENGINEER/HYDROLOGIST:** UMA Engineering, Dyregrov Consultants

**LIFE SAFETY:** Leber Rubes: Jonathan Rubes, David Syrett

**BUILDING ENVELOPE:** Brook Van Dalen & Associates: Mark Brook

**MICROCLIMATE:** RWDI: Duncan Phillips, Frank Kriksic

**QUANTITY SURVEYOR:** Hanscomb

**MUNICIPAL AND SITE SERVICES:** Wardrop Engineering

**TRAFFIC/ACCESS/PARKING ENGINEER:** ND LEA Engineers & Planners

**WATER FEATURE CONSULTANT:** Dan Euser Waterarchitecture

**MODEL PHOTOGRAPHY:** Tom Arban, Robert Hill, John Peterson

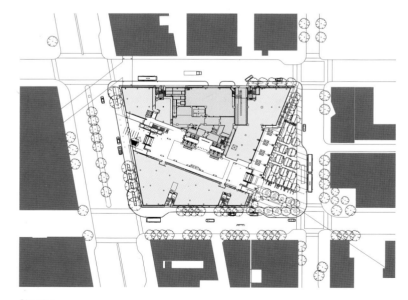

Site plan

OPPOSITE
South facade

The Manitoba Hydro Downtown Office Project (DTOP) maximizes the natural resources of its downtown Winnipeg site to establish a model for cold-climate design. The 700,000 square-foot facility houses 2,000 employees in a twenty-two-story tower. Its three-story podium base covers an entire urban block and contains retail and lobby spaces accessible to the public.

The morphology of the building is driven by solar and prevailing-wind orientations. Winnipeg receives more sun than any other large Canadian city and thus the A-configuration of the building opens to the south to receive sun and prevailing winds from the south with stacked atria that collect light, fresh air, and smaller communities of employees. Each floor of the eighteen-story tower is divided into groups organized around six-story atria, each with independent air inputs and exhaust. Each leg of the A contains column-free office loft space, raised access floors, and exposed concrete ceilings. The design provides maximum flexibility and optimal heating and cooling strategies while also ensuring adaptability to future change and use. The vertex of the A on the north also contains stacked three-story atria and is flanked by a solar chimney, the building's primary air-exhaust device. The solar chimney is partitioned with fire and smoke dampers into three primary zones, connected to each atria level. A solar-gain collector at the top of the chimney accelerates the stack effect. Partitioning any air-stack strategies with shut-off dampers is essential to meeting North American code requirements without relying upon more elaborate fire control systems.

The key energy strategies for this building are maximum daylight and 100 percent fresh air. Fresh air in cold climates requires supplemental heating of the intake air. In this case, fresh air is drawn through each south atrium where the sun preheats the air. Water walls in the south atria humidify winter supply air and dehumidify supply air in the summer. Fan-coil units with fire dampers blow the fresh air in to the raised floor plenum. Ventilation-floor displacement air diffusers distribute the air, and the exhaust air from each floor is collected in the north atria. In the summer, the spent air exhausts through the top of the solar chimney and in the winter the warmed exhaust air is recirculated through the parking garage. Operable inner leaf windows allow for localized, individual climate control in the offices. The building envelope controls solar gains with automated shading louvers in the double-glazed facade where the solar-control device is protected. The south facade of the atria also have operable louvers that close in the summer to minimize solar-heat gains. Geothermal heating and cooling supplies the hydronic ceiling and tempers the operative temperature of each office slab while minimizing power demand.

The client required the C-2000 Integrated Design Process (IDP), a specific design method developed by Natural Resources Canada's CANMET Energy Technology Center. The process requires architects, clients, and expert consultants to participate in initial integrated-design workshops to gain investment from the start and to imbue early design decisions with information-rich content with the objective of swerving the design toward integrated solutions. The Manitoba Hydro project demonstrates the value of the IDP by achieving a clear model for energy-efficient building design in an extremely cold, dry climate.

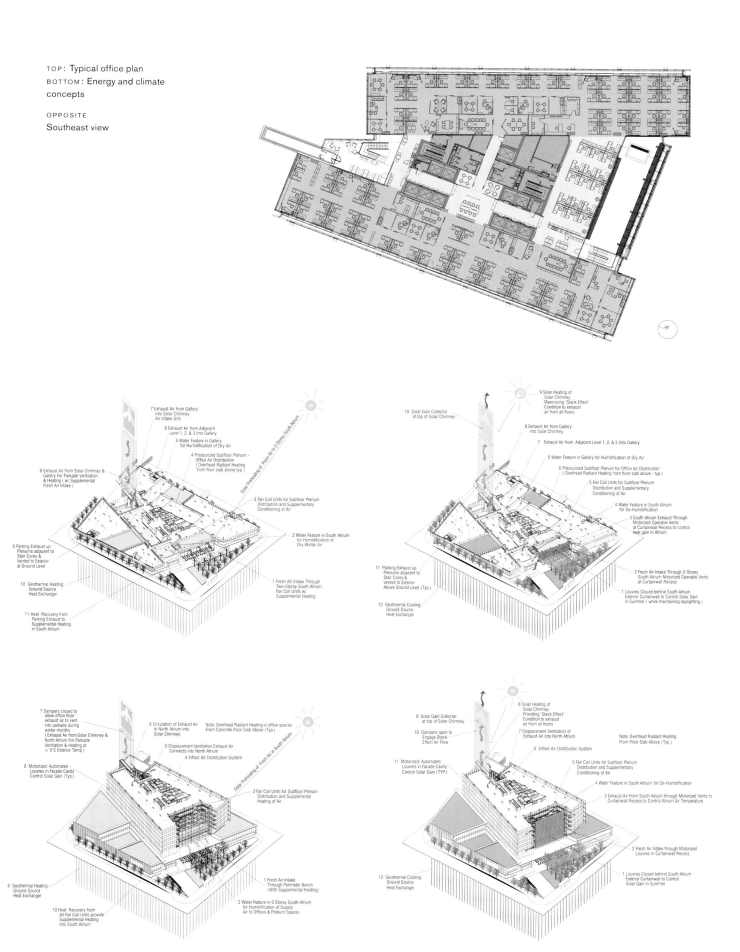

TOP: Typical office plan
BOTTOM: Energy and climate concepts

OPPOSITE
Southeast view

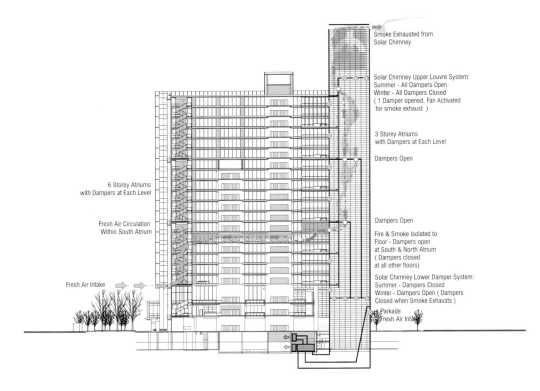

Smoke Exhausted from
Solar Chimney

Solar Chimney Upper Louvre System:
Summer - All Dampers Open
Winter - All Dampers Closed
( 1 Damper opened, Fan Activated
for smoke exhaust )

3 Storey Atriums
with Dampers at Each Level

Dampers Open

6 Storey Atriums
with Dampers at Each Level

Fresh Air Circulation
Within South Atrium

Dampers Open

Fire & Smoke Isolated to
Floor - Dampers open
at South & North Atrium
( Dampers closed
at all other floors)

Solar Chimney Lower Damper System:
Summer - Dampers Closed
Winter - Dampers Open ( Dampers
Closed when Smoke Exhausts )

Fresh Air Intake

Parkade
Fresh Air Intake

TOP: Airflow zoning and
dampening
BOTTOM: North facade day
and night

OPPOSITE
TOP: Southern-facing atria
BOTTOM: Typical office
interior

# The Bank of America Tower at One Bryant Park

New York, New York

———

Cook + Fox Architects, New York, New York

**ARCHITECT:** Cook + Fox Architects: Richard A. Cook, Partner; Robert F. Fox, Jr., Partner; Serge Appel, Associate Partner; Mark Rusitzky, Senior Associate; Associates Mark A. Squeo, Daniel K. Berry, Pamela Campbell, Carlos Fighetti, Matt Fischesser, Caroline Hahn, Tobias Holler, Ethan Lu, Natalia Martinez, Lisa Storer, Jesus Tordecilla, Ife Vanable, Arzan S. Wadia

**EXECUTIVE ARCHITECT:** Adamson Associates Architects
**STRUCTURAL ENGINEER:** Severud Associates
**MECHANICAL ENGINEER:** Jaros, Baum & Bolles
**GEOTECHNICAL ENGINEER:** Mueser Rutledge Consulting Engineers
**LIGHTING CONSULTANT:** Cline Bettridge Bernstein Lighting Design
**CODE CONSULTANT:** JAM Consultants
**BASE BUILDING ACOUSTICIAN:** Shen Milsom & Wilke
**THEATER ACOUSTICIANS:** JaffeHolden Acoustics
**THEATER CONSULTANT:** Fisher Dachs Associates
**ELEVATOR CONSULTANT:** VDA
**CONSTRUCTION MANAGER:** Tishman Construction Corporation
**EXTERIOR WALL CONSULTANT:** Israel Berger & Associates
**SECURITY CONSULTANT:** Ducibella Venter & Santore
**EXTERIOR MAINTENANCE CONSULTANT:** Entek Engineering
**NYC TRANSIT CONSULTANT:** Vollmer Associates
**HISTORIC CONSULTANT:** Higgins & Quasebarth
**ENERGY/ENVIRONMENTAL CONSULTANT:** Steven Winter Associates
**SOLAR DESIGN/PHOTOVOLTAIC CONSULTANT:** Solar Design Associates
**WIND CONSULTANT:** altPOWER
**DEVELOPERS:** the Durst Organization and Bank of America.

strategy facilitates greater individual control and response to local conditions. Carbon dioxide sensors adjust fresh air ventilation based upon local, current room air conditions rather than predetermined air exchanges per hour for the whole building. At the core of the building's energy system is a 4.6 mega-watt natural gas-fired cogeneration plant. The plant supplies steam and electricity for the building. During the night, the plant produces ice for cooling loads the following day, offsetting electrical demand during the days.

The building also captures and reuses almost all of its stormwater and gray water in 329,000-gallon tanks. Waterless urinals and low-flow toilet and sink fixtures throughout the building, along with the storm- and gray-water systems, will save ten million gallons of water annually.

This project will be the first LEED platinum high rise tower.

The 945-foot-tall Bank of America Tower is located at Forty-second Street and Sixth Avenue in Manhattan, opposite Bryant Park. The 2,200,000-square-foot tower was developed as a joint venture between the Durst Organization and the Bank of America. As its New York headquarters, Bank of America will occupy three-quarters of the building. The base of the tower creates a variety of important public spaces, including the restored Henry Miller Theater on Forty-third Street. It also provides three times the public circulation space of a typical as-of-right office building, including an urban garden room and a new entrance to the Times Square subway station.

The integrated strategies for this high-rise building focus on daylighting and indoor air quality that foster human comfort and employee productivity. The double-glazed envelope consists of floor-to-ceiling low-iron, low-E glazing for maximum transparency and thermal performance. The raised floor plenum contains a filtered displacement system fed by floor-by-floor air-handling units. This decentralized

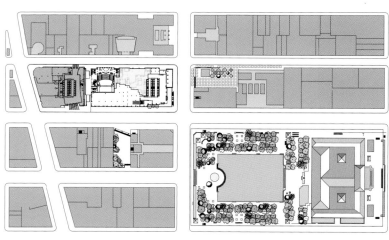

Site plan

OPPOSITE
Rendering of tower

24

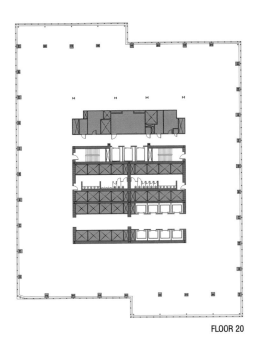

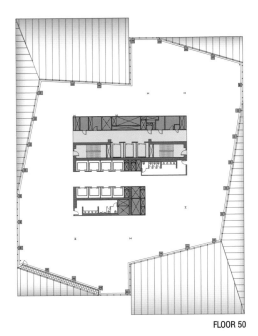

FLOOR 20

FLOOR 50

TOP: Typical office floor plans
BOTTOM: Tower throughout
a day

OPPOSITE
TOP: Water and air diagrams
BOTTOM: Rendering at
street level

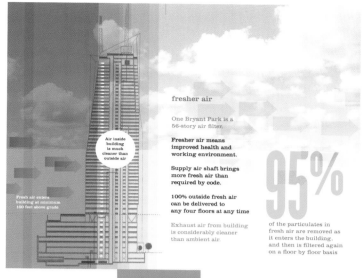

### fresher air

One Bryant Park is a 56-story air filter.

Fresher air means improved health and working environment.

Supply air shaft brings more fresh air than required by code.

100% outside fresh air can be delivered to any four floors at any time

Exhaust air from building is considerably cleaner than ambient air.

Air inside building is much cleaner than outside air

Fresh air enters building at minimum 100 feet above grade

## 95%

of the particulates in fresh air are removed as it enters the building, and then is filtered again on a floor by floor basis

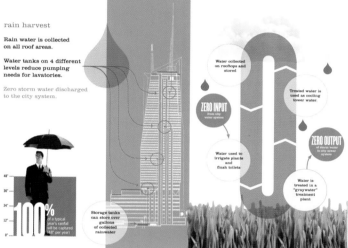

### rain harvest

Rain water is collected on all roof areas.

Water tanks on 4 different levels reduce pumping needs for lavatories.

Zero storm water discharged to the city system.

## 100%

of a typical year's rainfall will be captured (48" per year)

Storage tanks can store over gallons of collected rainwater

Water collected on rooftops and stored

**ZERO INPUT** from city water system

Treated water is used as cooling tower water.

Water used to irrigate plants and flush toilets

Water is treated in a "graywater" treatment plant

**ZERO OUTPUT** of storm water to city sewer system

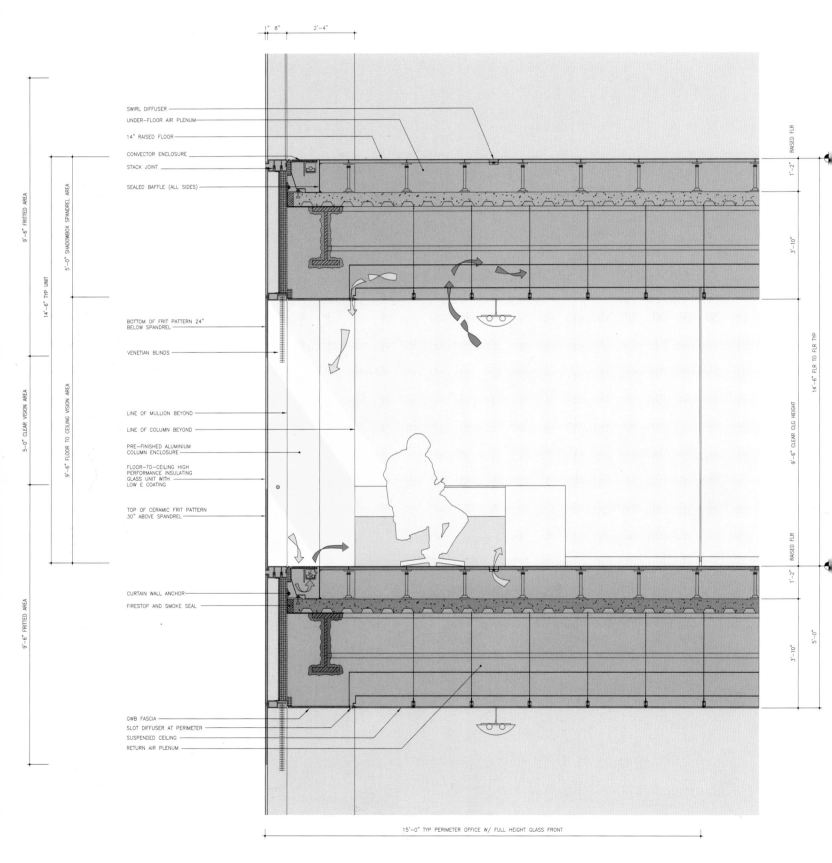

9'-6" FRITED AREA

14'-6" TYP UNIT

5'-0" SHADOWBOX SPANDREL AREA

5'-0" CLEAR VISION AREA

9'-6" FLOOR TO CEILING VISION AREA

9'-6" FRITED AREA

1" 8" 2'-4"

SWIRL DIFFUSER
UNDER-FLOOR AIR PLENUM
14" RAISED FLOOR
CONVECTOR ENCLOSURE
STACK JOINT
SEALED BAFFLE (ALL SIDES)

BOTTOM OF FRIT PATTERN 24"
BELOW SPANDREL

VENETIAN BLINDS

LINE OF MULLION BEYOND
LINE OF COLUMN BEYOND
PRE-FINISHED ALUMINIUM
COLUMN ENCLOSURE
FLOOR-TO-CEILING HIGH
PERFORMANCE INSULATING
GLASS UNIT WITH
LOW E COATING

TOP OF CERAMIC FRIT PATTERN
30" ABOVE SPANDREL

CURTAIN WALL ANCHOR
FIRESTOP AND SMOKE SEAL

GWB FASCIA
SLOT DIFFUSER AT PERIMETER
SUSPENDED CEILING
RETURN AIR PLENUM

RAISED FLR

1'-2"

3'-10"

14'-6" FLR TO FLR TYP

9'-6" CLEAR CLG HEIGHT

RAISED FLR

1'-2"

3'-10"

5'-0"

15'-0" TYP PERIMETER OFFICE W/ FULL HEIGHT GLASS FRONT

29

# Lovejoy Building

Portland, Oregon

OPSIS Architecture, Portland, Oregon

ARCHITECT AND OWNER: Opsis Architecture
STRUCTURAL ENGINEER: DCI Engineers
MECHANICAL ENGINEER: Interface Engineering
ELECTRICAL ENGINEER: James D. Graham & Associates
TELECOM CONSULTANT: Mark Day & Associates
ELECTRICAL SUBCONTRACTOR: Greenway Electric
MECHANICAL SUBCONTRACTOR: Hunter Davisson
SUSTAINABILITY CONSULTANT: Brightworks
GENERAL CONTRACTOR: Gray Purcell
FINISH CONTRACTOR: Shipman Construction
STEEL FABRICATION: Madden Fabrication
WINDOW PROVIDER: JELD-WEN
The project is LEED Gold certified and the addition
is designed as LEED Platinum.

The Lovejoy Building in Portland, Oregon, is a renovation of the 1910 Marshall Wells Stable Building, a brick masonry building in Portland's northwest "Slabtown" area served by Portland's downtown streetcar system. The building houses the offices of Opsis Architecture on the upper floor and a sports apparel company on the lower floor. The architects have begun work on an expansion and vertical addition to the building, as well, that accommodates the growth of both tenants. The initial renovation strategically anticipates the future addition.

The renovation by and for the architects' office is essentially a laboratory of various techniques that apply to integrated design in all their work. The experiments abound. Bricks that were extracted to enlarge the window opening for more daylight are used in the garage as porous pavers that allow leakage from bikes and cars to trickle back into the ground. Twenty photovoltaic panels on the roof generate 2,400 watts of electricity for the office's use. However, many of the strategies are less visible but yield greater effects.

The retrofit of the existing 1910 load-bearing brick structure required a major seismic upgrade. The architects used the renovation as an opportunity for an integrated response to advanced structural upgrades, enhanced user thermal comfort, and improved energy performance. The solution was to add to the thermal mass of the building with new poured-in-place, high fly-ash concrete perimeter walls and a new concrete floor system. An in-floor cross-linked polyethylene (PEX) pipe hydronic system was selected to provide the building's primary heating and cooling system, coupled with an integrated natural ventilation strategy using windows, skylights, and ventilators. In the winter, water runs through the thermal mass, creating a stable temperature range and maximizing user comfort while introducing heat low in the space. Fan noise and air drafts have also been eliminated. In the summer, radiant cooling is provided through two primary strategies. The renovation is designed for a night purge with ventilation that exchanges the heat gains of the previous day with cool night air, leaving the space cool for the next morning. The radiant slab system is also employed in the cooling activities by collecting heat out of the slab, running the water through a rooftop chiller where the heat is evacuated, and then cool water is returned back though the in-slab piping system. The cooling cycle operates with a significantly tighter temperature delta, requiring closer pipe spacing, and includes monitors to hold the dew point below the point of condensation. The radiant-cooling strategy significantly lowers the operative temperature that a body perceives, and the system performance has been enhanced by the inclusion of user-controlled ceiling fans throughout the space. The radiant strategy requires significantly less space for equivalent heating and cooling, minimizing material and energy-intensive forced-air systems. Radiant strategies also have the benefit of less recirculated air, further improving air quality and human comfort.

Other strategies include milling extracted wood joists for reuse as stair risers and treads. Various low-flow plumbing fixtures were specified to not only lower water consumption but also offer an opportunity to directly test their performance and durability. The office space was modeled for uniform natural balanced daylight using a heliodon as a lighting laboratory. Although daylighting and operable windows constitute the primary energy systems, power-operated systems are controlled by a building management system and sensors. The digital system modulates lighting according to levels, with zoned photocell sensors located on the open office ceiling. Automated sunshades on the west face of the building are controlled by

Physical context

photocells set to an astronomical clock and block unwanted light and heat gains. Carbon dioxide sensors in the office help control the amount of required ventilation in the space. Ceiling fans are located throughout the open studio and improve human comfort perceptions with less energy and sound than typical forced-air systems.

The renovations were designed with a proposed addition in mind. Renovation skylights were placed where proposed structural columns will be located and the skylights are then to be reused in the addition roof. In other cases, steel columns have already been placed to receive the new proposed structural columns. The new additions will double the size of the original building. The addition extends the logic of the air, water, light, and heat energy strategies of the renovation, using a new stair core as a buoyant stack. A vegetated roof and water cistern will manage stormwater on site. In both the renovation and addition, the integrated design focuses on the integration of an existing building's inherent qualities for a "structural solution." There is an assumption in this approach that the material, energy, and water available on any given site, including that embedded in existing buildings, is sufficient for human comfort and compelling spaces.

Renovation process and plans

OPPOSITE
Interior views

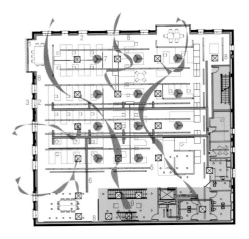

1 sliding glass doors w/ guardrail
2 automated casement & awning windows
3 west facing automated exterior shades
4 automated operable skylights
5 automated dimmable lighting tied to
6 daylight sensors
7 displacement air system
8 ceiling fans
9 7" thick interior concrete shell for thermal mass & structural shear resistance stack ventilation through main stair

SECOND FLOOR REFLECTED CEILING PLAN

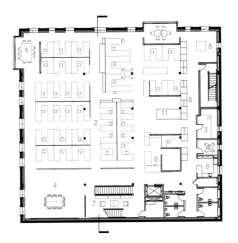

1 entry
2 open office
3 private office
4 conference room
5 circulating art gallery
6 reception area
7 lounge
8 library
9 kitchenette
10 workshop
11 copy/work area
12 car, electric scooter & bike storage
13 taxi depot
14 taxi parking
15 streetcar

SECOND FLOOR PLAN

N.W. LOVEJOY STREET

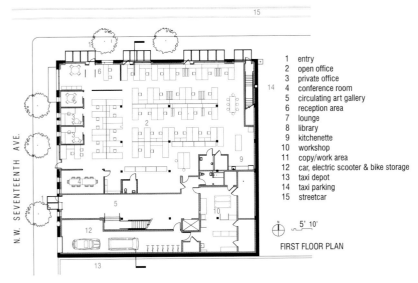

N.W. SEVENTEENTH AVE.

1 entry
2 open office
3 private office
4 conference room
5 circulating art gallery
6 reception area
7 lounge
8 library
9 kitchenette
10 workshop
11 copy/work area
12 car, electric scooter & bike storage
13 taxi depot
14 taxi parking
15 streetcar

5' 10'

FIRST FLOOR PLAN

TOP, MIDDLE: Sunshade operations
BOTTOM: Renovated apertures

OPPOSITE
TOP: Wall sections
BOTTOM: Renovated apertures

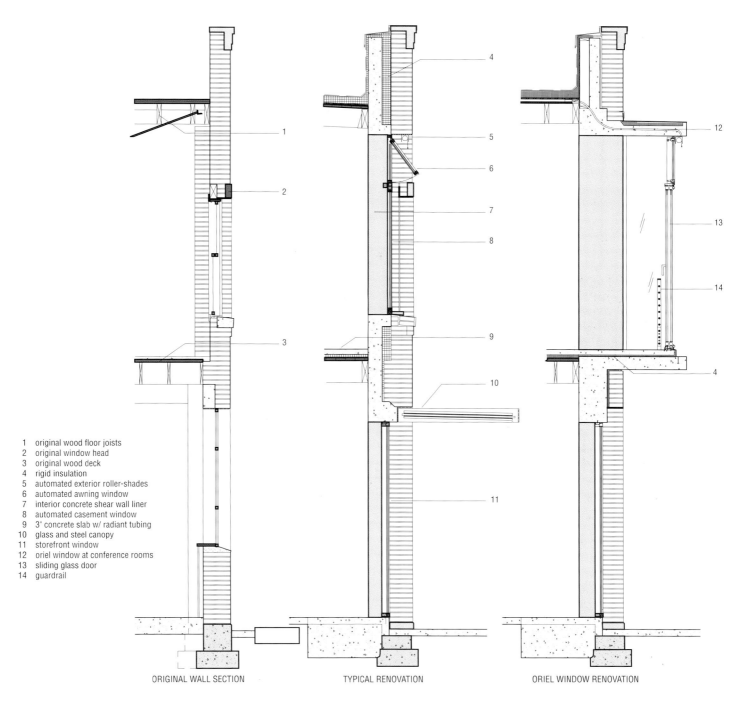

1   original wood floor joists
2   original window head
3   original wood deck
4   rigid insulation
5   automated exterior roller-shades
6   automated awning window
7   interior concrete shear wall liner
8   automated casement window
9   3" concrete slab w/ radiant tubing
10  glass and steel canopy
11  storefront window
12  oriel window at conference rooms
13  sliding glass door
14  guardrail

ORIGINAL WALL SECTION        TYPICAL RENOVATION        ORIEL WINDOW RENOVATION

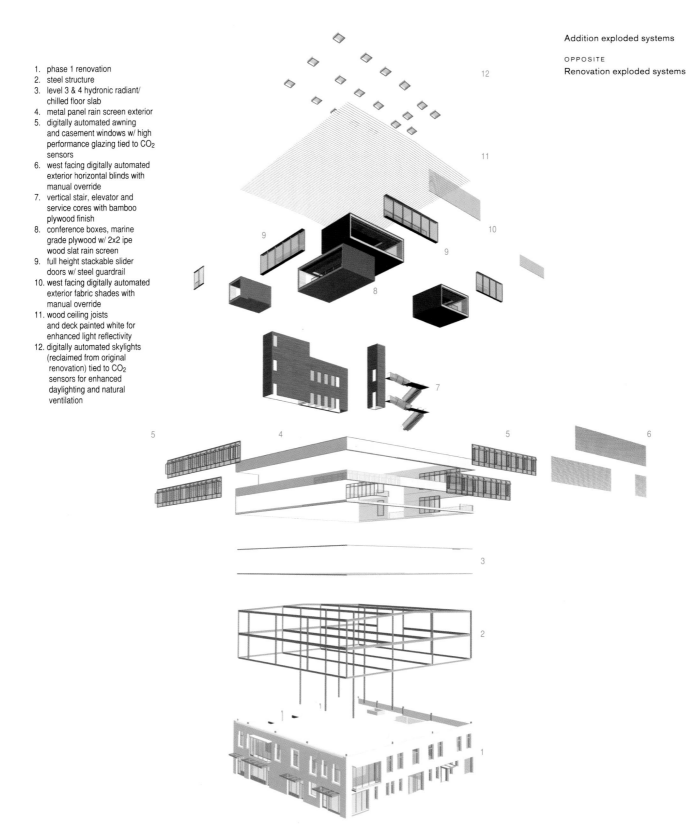

1. phase 1 renovation
2. steel structure
3. level 3 & 4 hydronic radiant/chilled floor slab
4. metal panel rain screen exterior
5. digitally automated awning and casement windows w/ high performance glazing tied to $CO_2$ sensors
6. west facing digitally automated exterior horizontal blinds with manual override
7. vertical stair, elevator and service cores with bamboo plywood finish
8. conference boxes, marine grade plywood w/ 2x2 ipe wood slat rain screen
9. full height stackable slider doors w/ steel guardrail
10. west facing digitally automated exterior fabric shades with manual override
11. wood ceiling joists and deck painted white for enhanced light reflectivity
12. digitally automated skylights (reclaimed from original renovation) tied to $CO_2$ sensors for enhanced daylighting and natural ventilation

Addition exploded systems

OPPOSITE

Renovation exploded systems

1. existing exterior brick shell; punched openings enlarged for enhanced daylighting and natural ventilation
2. digitally automated awning and casement windows w/ high performance glazing tied to $CO_2$ sensors
3. west facing digitally automated exterior fabric shades with manual override
4. interior concrete shell liner added for shear resistance and radiant building mass
5. full height cantilevered concrete oriels w/ slider doors and guardrails
6. level 2 hydronic radiant / chilled floor slab
7. existing timber post and beam structure
8. steel columns embedded in interior concrete shell liner for future 2-story expansion
9. vertical stair and elevator cores with bamboo plywood finish
10. interior partitions
11. existing wood ceiling joists and deck painted white for enhanced light reflectivity
12. digitally automated skylights tied to $CO_2$ sensors for enhanced daylighting and natural ventilation

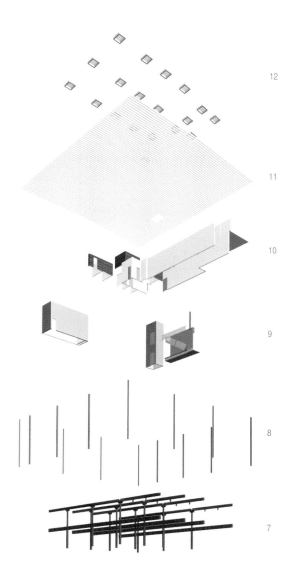

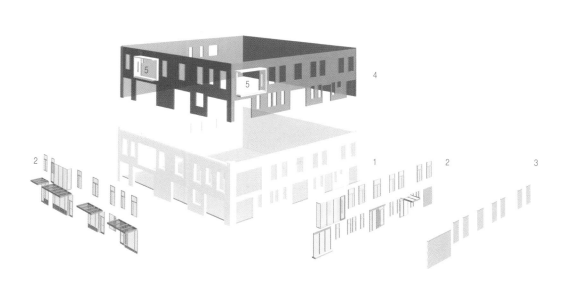

1 automated windows
2 automated skylights
3 photovoltaic arrays
4 radiant concrete slabs
5 ceiling fans
6 displacement air system
7 ecoroof
8 stack ventilation thru main stair
9 water catchment basin
10 streetcar
11 electric scooter charging
 & bike storage
12 taxi depot

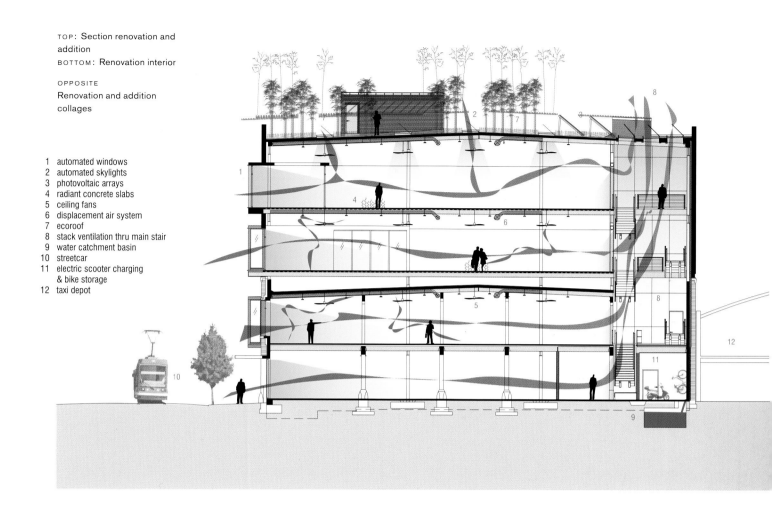

# 290 Mulberry

New York, New York

———

SHoP Architects, New York, New York

**ARCHITECT:** SHoP Architects
Christopher R. Sharples, William W.Sharples, Coren
D. Sharples, Kimberly J. Holden, Gregg A. Pasquarelli,
Principals; Federico Negro, Project Manager; Nash
Hurley, Steve Sanderson, Tyler Goss, Takeshi Tornier,
Project Team
**CLIENT/OWNER/DEVELOPER:** Cardinal Real Estate
Investments
**STRUCTURAL ENGINEER:** Robert Silman Associates
**MEP ENGINEER:** Laszlo Bodak Engineer
**GENERAL CONTRACTOR:** KISKA Group
**PRECAST FABRICATION:** Architectural Polymers (liner),
Saramac (precasting)

The thirteen-story, 27,000-square-foot building at the corner
of Mulberry and Houston Streets, contains retail space on
the ground floor and nine residential units above. The site
is located in a special zoning district, requiring masonry
cladding along street walls. A specific code parameter
permitting architectural ornamentation to break the plane
of the building envelope at 10 percent for every 100 square
feet is the origin of this undulating masonry pattern. The
design approach overtly merges such zoning regulations
with fabrication requirements, and makes use of parametric
and BIM software as a means of controling information in
defining this precast masonry building envelope.

The architects worked parametrically at two concurrent
scales—brick and panel—to optimize the exterior envelope.
At the scale of the brick, the intent was to maximize the
allowable undulating geometry, while minimizing the
overall thickness of the wall. For proper fabrication, no
single brick could push beyond its neighbor more than
three-quarters of an inch. The parametric design software
GenerativeComponents was used to model and verify this
approach.

At another scale—the masonry panel—the architects
optimized the assembly of the precast curtain wall. The
database and model in the software program Digital Project
was used to define this assembly. Information from each
scale fed into a model in the program Autodesk Revit,
from which all construction documents for the project
were issued. The sequence of software is as important to
the design as the sequence of final assembly. Information
derived in GenerativeComponents fed into the parts
modeled in Digital Project. These parts in turn defined
the object families in Revit. Although the software itself is
admittedly not interoperable and often requires additional
manual work for the designer, here the software was used
to integrate a range of pragmatic parameters to yield a new
interpretation of masonry detailing and ornament.

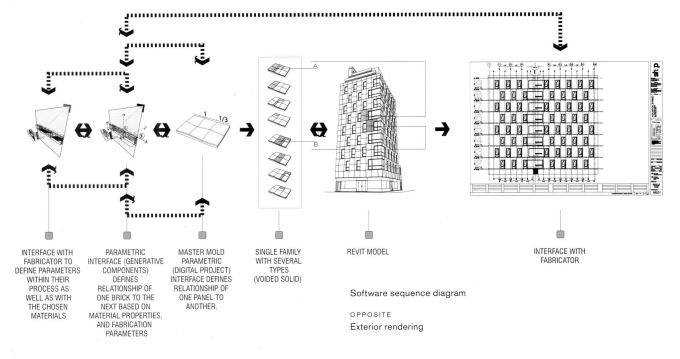

INTERFACE WITH
FABRICATOR TO
DEFINE PARAMETERS
WITHIN THEIR
PROCESS AS
WELL AS WITH
THE CHOSEN
MATERIALS

PARAMETRIC
INTERFACE (GENERATIVE
COMPONENTS)
DEFINES
RELATIONSHIP OF
ONE BRICK TO THE
NEXT BASED ON
MATERIAL PROPERTIES,
AND FABRICATION
PARAMETERS

MASTER MOLD
PARAMETRIC
(DIGITAL PROJECT)
INTERFACE DEFINES
RELATIONSHIP OF
ONE PANEL TO
ANOTHER.

SINGLE FAMILY
WITH SEVERAL
TYPES
(VOIDED SOLID)

REVIT MODEL

INTERFACE WITH
FABRICATOR

Software sequence diagram

OPPOSITE
Exterior rendering

A key component of the assembly is the one that will not be installed with the masonry panels. A rubber piece of formwork, formliner, will hold the brick in place as the concrete portion of each panel is poured. The architects worked with the fabricator to translate and fabricate the geometry that defines the master mold. This mold then is used to fabricate all of the formliners necessary to create every panel in the building.

The focus here is on a design process that deliberately integrates key parameters of a building assembly early in the process as a driver and enabler of novelty. This inherently requires critical input from material fabricators and installers. As such, the composition of the building, the material, and the design/fabrication team are developed with equal rigor. In this case, the role of the architect is one of capturing and channeling information to promote innovation in both process and product.

Plan geometries

OPPOSITE
TOP: Wall sections
BOTTOM: Panel elevation
diagram

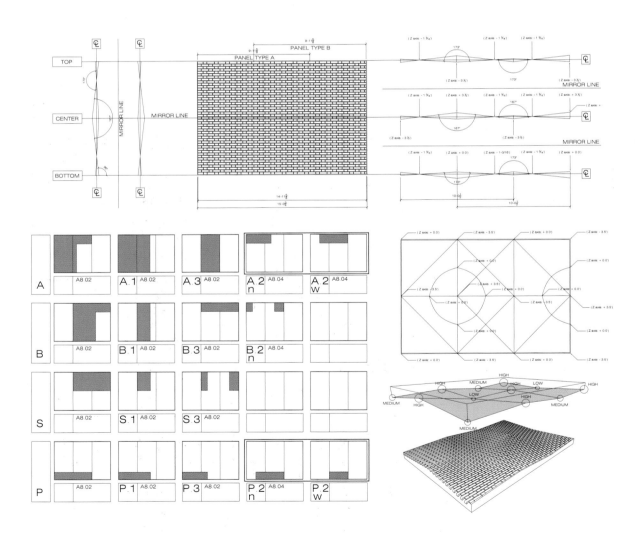

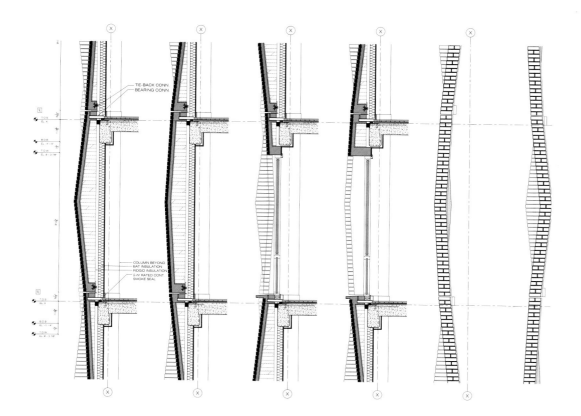

TIE-BACK CONN
BEARING CONN

COLUMN BEYOND
BAT INSULATION
RIGID INSULATION
2-hr RATED CONT
SMOKE SEAL

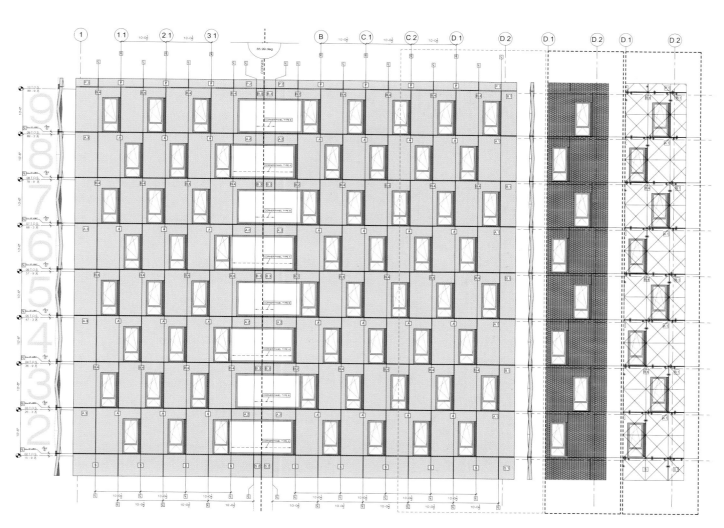

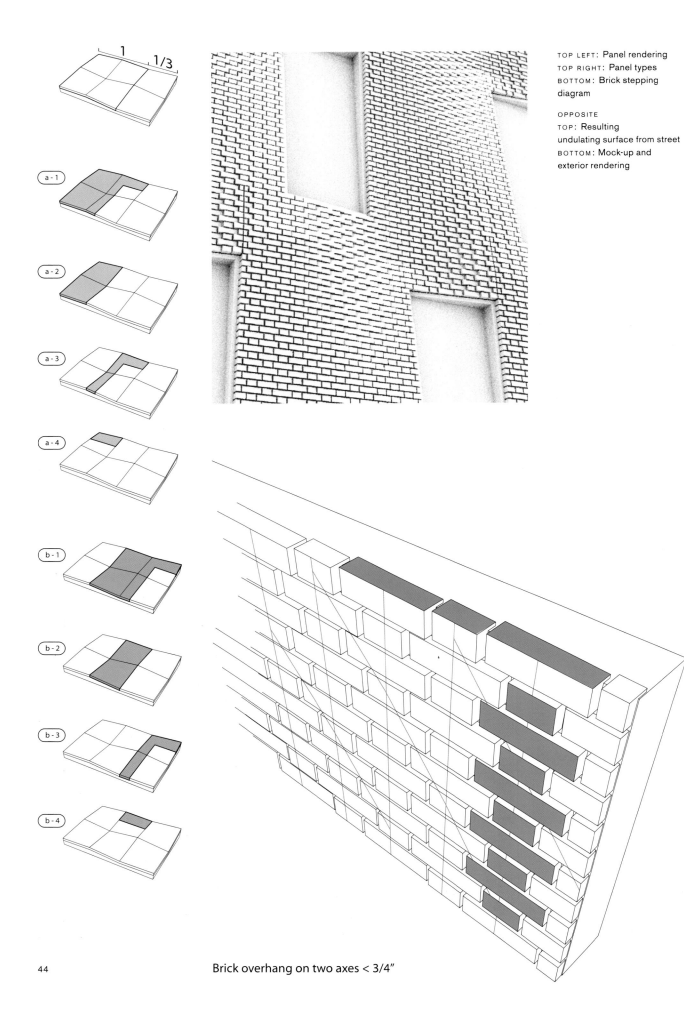

1    1/3

a - 1
a - 2
a - 3
a - 4

b - 1
b - 2
b - 3
b - 4

Brick overhang on two axes < 3/4"

TOP LEFT: Panel rendering
TOP RIGHT: Panel types
BOTTOM: Brick stepping
diagram

OPPOSITE
TOP: Resulting
undulating surface from street
BOTTOM: Mock-up and
exterior rendering

# The Clarence

Kingston, Ontario, Canada

---

Behnisch Architects, Venice, California, and Next Phase Studios, Boston, Massachusetts

ARCHITECT: Behnisch Architects and Next Phase Studios
ARCHITECT OF RECORD: Shoalts and Zaback Architects
STRUCTURAL ENGINEER: Yolles Partnership
MEP: Keen Engineering
ENVIRONMENTAL ENGINEER: Transsolar Energietechnik GmbH
COST CONSULTANT: Curran Mccabe Ravindran Ross, Inc.
CLIENT: Kincore Holdings

The Clarence provides a compelling example of an approach that integrates a variety of uses and public space along with air, light, and energy strategies that align to meet the needs of contemporary cities and housing. The result is a robust, vital, and highly marketable housing solution.

The Clarence, a forty-two-unit mixed-use housing block, fills a vacant parcel in the center of Kingston, Ontario. The building works to complete the urban fabric but also attempts to draw people into a courtyard situated in the interior of the parcel. The courtyard pushes building massing toward the street edge, completing the urban front along Clarence Street and Brock Street. At the street level, the inner courtyard atrium and interior retail is accessed by passages from Clarence and Brock streets. The massing, however, steps back at the adjacent parapet height according to allowable zoning. The step backs provide several roof decks and vegetated roofs for the housing units. The solar shading studies of the massing demonstrate that no significant overshadowing on adjacent buildings will occur, except during the low light in December.

The air, light, and energy strategies inherent in an atrium scheme help organize the building section. The shared corridors are organized around the atrium's central light well. This provides natural light and expands the perception of otherwise confined corridors with visual connections in plan and section. Also evident in the section, the building uses concrete as structure, thermal-mass energy transfer, and finish materials. The floor slabs use radiant heat and cooling connected to geothermal energy sources. Mechanical ventilation is tempered by a ground duct that preheats or precools fresh air intake. Exhaust in the winter draws down to a centralized heat exchanger in the three below-grade parking levels, warming intake air. In the summer, exhaust air from the units and the atrium are exhausted at the top of the building through buoyancy.

The units utilize a "winter garden" buffer space off of each living space. The buffer allows the space to be used as a balcony in the summer, a thermal buffer in the winter, and additional living space in temperate times of the year. Operable, shaped solar-control louvers in the buffer space function as a light shelf, directing daylight further into the depth of each unit. The buffer space and operable windows provide fresh air.

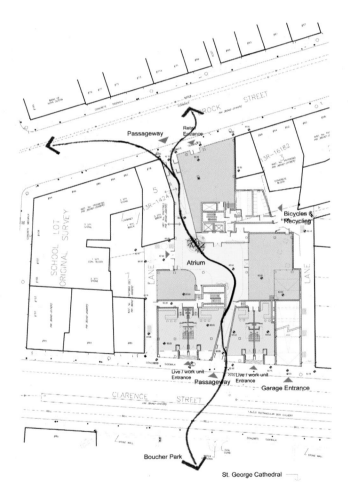

Site plan

OPPOSITE
TOP: Elevation
BOTTOM: View from Boucher Park

Penthouse A

Penthouse B

Solar Collectors          Solar Collectors    Roof Terrace

Terrace

Balcony                                  Balcony

Terrace                                  Terrace

Terrace    Wintergarden

Wintergarden

Garage Door

Entrance to          Passage      Entrance to          82.80
Live Work Units                    Live Work Units        STREET

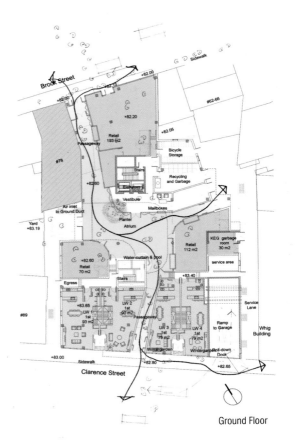

Ground Floor

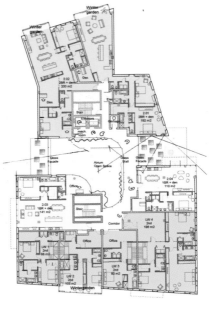

Level Two

Level Three

Level Five

Level Eight

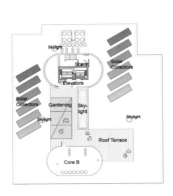

Roof Plan

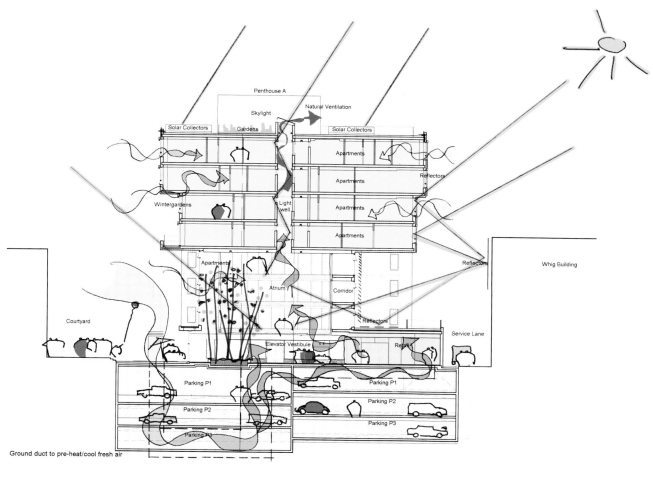

Penthouse A
Skylight
Natural Ventilation
Solar Collectors
Gardens
Solar Collectors
Apartments
Reflectors
Apartments
Light well
Wintergardens
Apartments
Apartments
Whig Building
Apartments
Atrium
Corridor
Reflectors
Courtyard
Elevator Vestibule
Retail A
Service Lane
Parking P1
Parking P1
Parking P2
Parking P2
Parking P3
Parking P3
Ground duct to pre-heat/cool fresh air

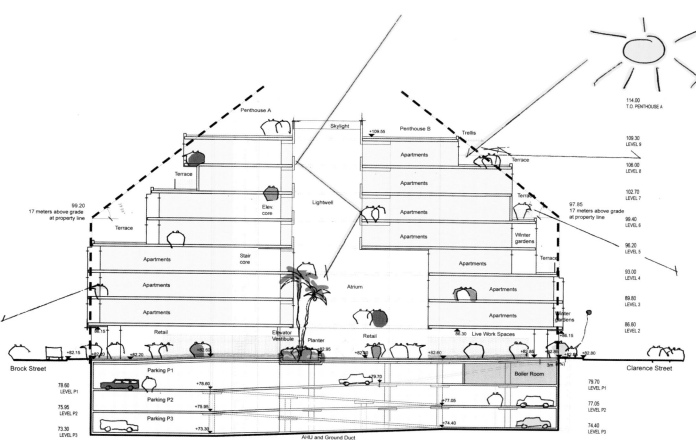

Penthouse A
Skylight
+109.55
Penthouse B
Trellis
114.00
T.O. PENTHOUSE A
Terrace
109.30
LEVEL 9
Apartments
Terrace
106.00
LEVEL 8
99.20
17 meters above grade
at property line
Elev. core
Lightwell
Apartments
Terrace
102.70
LEVEL 7
97.85
17 meters above grade
at property line
Terrace
Apartments
Winter gardens
99.40
LEVEL 6
96.20
LEVEL 5
Stair core
Apartments
Apartments
Terrace
93.00
LEVEL 4
Apartments
Atrium
Apartments
89.80
LEVEL 3
86.15
Apartments
Winter gardens
Apartments
86.60
LEVEL 2
Retail
Elevator Vestibule
Planter
Retail
86.30
Live Work Spaces
+86.15
+82.15
Brock Street
+82.20
+82.20
+82.85
+82.95
+82.80
+82.60
+82.85
+82.80
3m
Clarence Street
78.60
LEVEL P1
Parking P1
+78.60
+79.70
Boiler Room
79.70
LEVEL P1
75.95
LEVEL P2
Parking P2
+75.95
+77.05
77.05
LEVEL P2
73.30
LEVEL P3
Parking P3
+73.30
+74.40
74.40
LEVEL P3
AHU and Ground Duct

North-South Section showing Passageway and Setbacks.

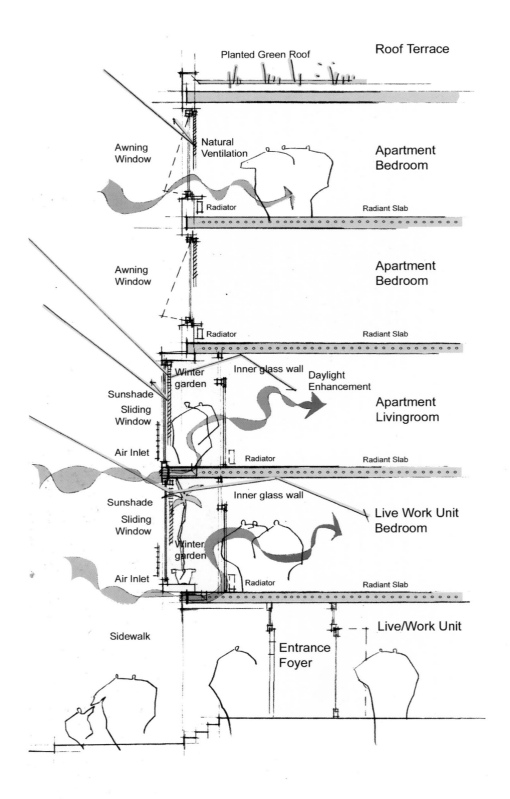

Planted Green Roof

Roof Terrace

Awning
Window

Natural
Ventilation

Apartment
Bedroom

Radiator

Radiant Slab

Awning
Window

Apartment
Bedroom

Radiator

Radiant Slab

Winter
garden

Inner glass wall

Daylight
Enhancement

Apartment
Livingroom

Sunshade
Sliding
Window

Air Inlet

Radiator

Radiant Slab

Inner glass wall

Live Work Unit
Bedroom

Sunshade
Sliding
Window

Winter
garden

Air Inlet

Radiator

Radiant Slab

Sidewalk

Live/Work Unit

Entrance
Foyer

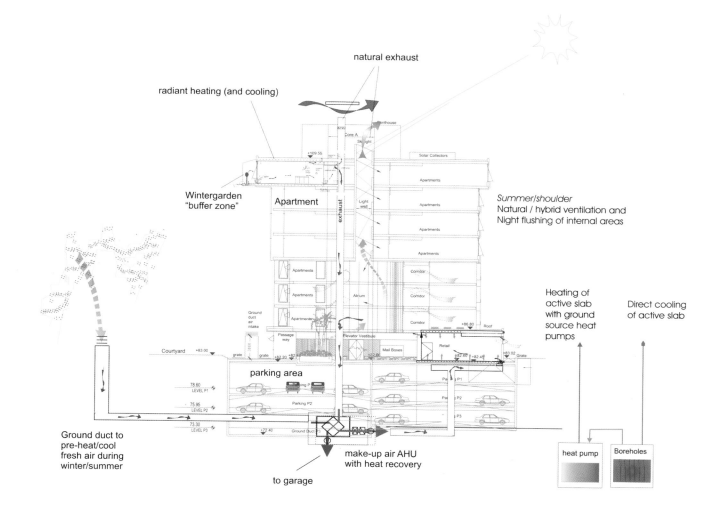

natural exhaust

radiant heating (and cooling)

Wintergarden "buffer zone"

Apartment

*Summer/shoulder*
Natural / hybrid ventilation and
Night flushing of internal areas

Heating of active slab with ground source heat pumps

Direct cooling of active slab

Courtyard +83.00

parking area

Ground duct to pre-heat/cool fresh air during winter/summer

make-up air AHU with heat recovery

to garage

heat pump    Boreholes

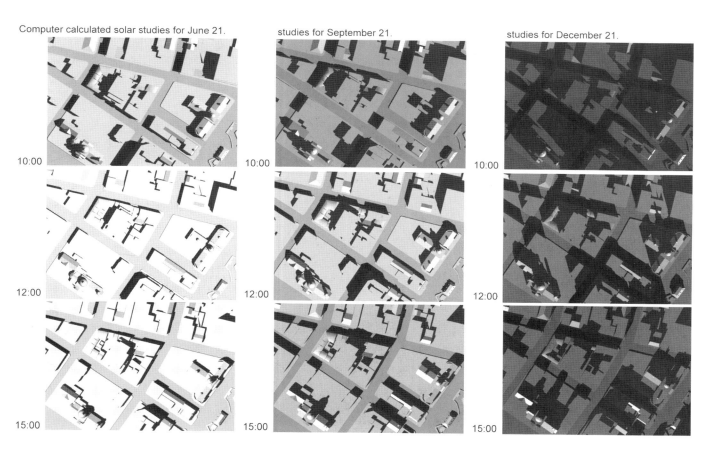

Computer calculated solar studies for June 21.          studies for September 21.          studies for December 21.

10:00          10:00          10:00

12:00          12:00          12:00

15:00          15:00          15:00

# 557/559

Boston, Massachusetts

---

Utile, Boston, Massachusetts

ARCHITECT: Utile
STRUCTURAL: Richmond So Engineer
MECHANICAL, ELECTRICAL, AND PLUMBING ENGINEER:
Verne G. Norman Associates, with South Shore
LANDSCAPE ARCHITECT: Michael Boucher Landscape
Architecture
GENERAL CONTRACTOR: RCG Builders
CLIENT: RCG
ENERGY STAR HOMES PROGRAM MANAGEMENT:
Conservation Services Group
This project is Energy Star® Homes 5-star qualified.

Utile is an architecture and urban design firm that looks for opportunities for design innovation within the regulatory, political, and economical constraints of market-oriented commissions. Compelled by a search for what they call the "pragmatic exception," the firm often finds territory for invention at the boundaries of building code classifications and through the creative deployment of off-the-shelf building systems.

Beyond code and construction, Utile engages the larger infrastructure of building production. For example, the firm has graphically reworked the U.S. Green Building Council (USGBC's) Leadership in Energy and Environmental Design (LEED) checklist to facilitate sustainable design choices early in the design process. Utile's strategic role in this area extends to a broader understanding of the design process as a cost-benefit analysis of the many choices required as a project unfolds. As a result, Utile is as much a strategic consulting firm as an architecture practice.

The 557/559 East Second Street residential development in South Boston is an example of Utile's approach. The project is comprised of eight new single-family row houses, located at the boundary of a small-scale working-class residential district and an industrial area. Two rows of four houses are organized around a linear dual-mode pedestrian and vehicular court. The row house configuration provides at least two exposures per floor; an advantage in terms of natural lighting and ventilation strategies.

As a result of the adjacent industrial landscape and opportunities for distant views of the Boston skyline, the typical row house section has been inverted, so that living areas are located above the bedrooms. To take advantage of views, light, and prevailing winds, the houses on the east side of the court have an additional half-floor of living space. In the east and west row, the houses have roof decks that look over adjacent buildings.

In Boston's highly competitive housing market, adopting a green strategy to appeal to twenty- and thirty-something "creative class" professionals was a central component of the development and design strategy. Within the economic constraints of market-rate housing, the project utilized a super-insulated building envelope with high-performance glazing, water-saving features such as dual-flush toilets, and environmentally sensitive material specifications including Energy Star appliances. Accordingly, "Live Contemporary, Live Green" was the project's tagline. Significantly, during the concurrent processes of design, marketing, and construction, the roles of the architect, broker, developer, and general contractor shifted and overlapped.

557/559 served as a pilot project for the Green Homes Northeast program. The organization's mission is to strategically transform the residential market so that energy-efficient, resource-efficient, and healthy housing becomes standard practice.

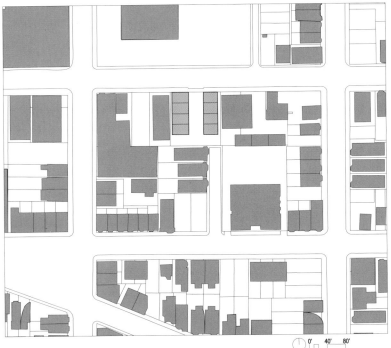

Site plan

OPPOSITE
Corner unit

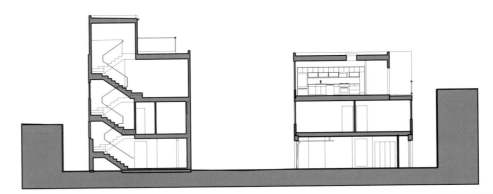

TOP: Elevations
MIDDLE: Section through court
BOTTOM: Court view

OPPOSITE
TOP: Street view
BOTTOM: Typical unit plans for 557/559

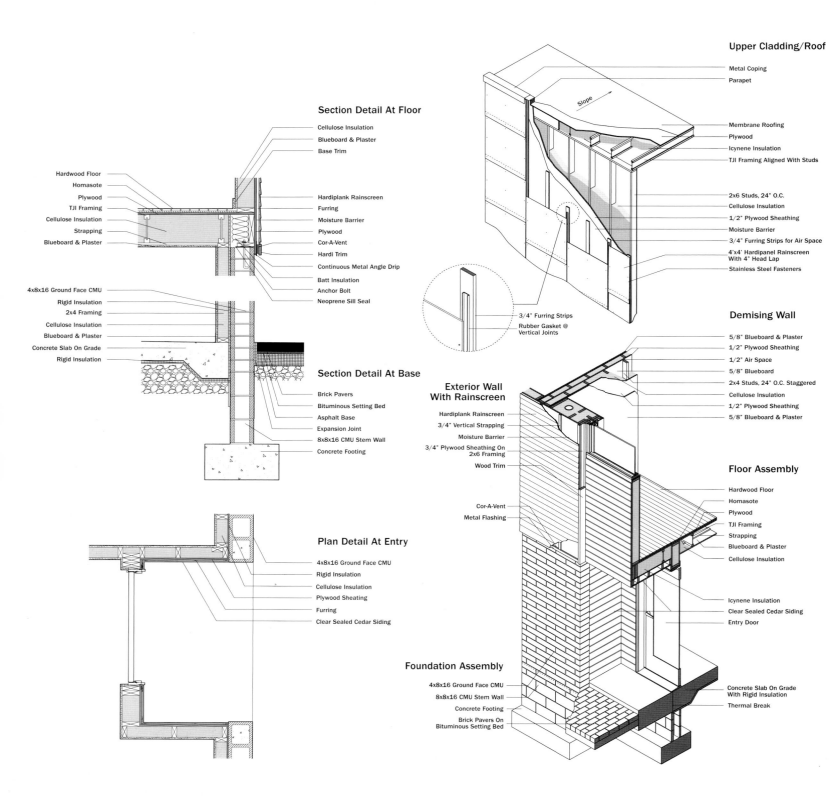

**Section Detail At Floor**

- Cellulose Insulation
- Blueboard & Plaster
- Base Trim

- Hardwood Floor
- Homasote
- Plywood
- TJI Framing
- Cellulose Insulation
- Strapping
- Blueboard & Plaster

- Hardiplank Rainscreen
- Furring
- Moisture Barrier
- Plywood
- Cor-A-Vent
- Hardi Trim
- Continuous Metal Angle Drip
- Batt Insulation
- Anchor Bolt
- Neoprene Sill Seal

- 4x8x16 Ground Face CMU
- Rigid Insulation
- 2x4 Framing
- Cellulose Insulation
- Blueboard & Plaster
- Concrete Slab On Grade
- Rigid Insulation

**Section Detail At Base**

- Brick Pavers
- Bituminous Setting Bed
- Asphalt Base
- Expansion Joint
- 8x8x16 CMU Stem Wall
- Concrete Footing

3/4" Furring Strips
Rubber Gasket @
Vertical Joints

**Plan Detail At Entry**

- 4x8x16 Ground Face CMU
- Rigid Insulation
- Cellulose Insulation
- Plywood Sheating
- Furring
- Clear Sealed Cedar Siding

**Upper Cladding/Roof**

- Metal Coping
- Parapet

Slope

- Membrane Roofing
- Plywood
- Icynene Insulation
- TJI Framing Aligned With Studs

- 2x6 Studs, 24" O.C.
- Cellulose Insulation
- 1/2" Plywood Sheathing
- Moisture Barrier
- 3/4" Furring Strips for Air Space
- 4'x4' Hardipanel Rainscreen With 4" Head Lap
- Stainless Steel Fasteners

**Demising Wall**

- 5/8" Blueboard & Plaster
- 1/2" Plywood Sheathing
- 1/2" Air Space
- 5/8" Blueboard
- 2x4 Studs, 24" O.C. Staggered
- Cellulose Insulation
- 1/2" Plywood Sheathing
- 5/8" Blueboard & Plaster

**Exterior Wall With Rainscreen**

- Hardiplank Rainscreen
- 3/4" Vertical Strapping
- Moisture Barrier
- 3/4" Plywood Sheathing On 2x6 Framing
- Wood Trim
- Cor-A-Vent
- Metal Flashing

**Floor Assembly**

- Hardwood Floor
- Homasote
- Plywood
- TJI Framing
- Strapping
- Blueboard & Plaster
- Cellulose Insulation
- Icynene Insulation
- Clear Sealed Cedar Siding
- Entry Door

**Foundation Assembly**

- 4x8x16 Ground Face CMU
- 8x8x16 CMU Stem Wall
- Concrete Footing
- Brick Pavers On Bituminous Setting Bed
- Concrete Slab On Grade With Rigid Insulation
- Thermal Break

# DDBC Model Residence One

Tucson, Arizona

John Folan and Mary Hardin, Tucson, Arizona

ARCHITECTS: John Folan and Mary Hardin
STRUCTURAL ENGINEER: David Jeeter, Steeler
MECHANICAL ENGINEER: Sadri Sabet
LANDSCAPE ARCHITECT: University of Arizona College of Architecture and Landscape Architecture
CONTRACTOR: Drachman Design-Build Coalition
OWNERS: Jose and Cecilia Perez
Text by John Folan

The College of Architecture and Landscape Architecture at the University of Arizona recently created the Drachman Design-Build Coalition (DDBC), a non-profit housing organization that offers technical expertise to the local community in an effort to produce prototypical, energy-efficient, low-cost dwellings. Each prototype is permitted as a model residence and the plans made available to non-profit and for-profit homebuilders with the intention of disseminating regionally specific design strategies to a broad audience. The first residence built under non-profit status, Residence One, is a rammed-earth and steel-frame dwelling that houses a family with an annual income below 80 percent of the mean household income for the Tucson metropolitan area. The college partnered with another local non-profit agent, Chicanos Por La Causa, to identify a low-income family and guide them through homeownership courses and budget counseling.

Residence One was designed by two professors, then drawn and constructed by architecture students. Although the design was developed with a high degree of specificity by the faculty members, there were opportunities for each student to contribute to the detailing of the materials assemblies, especially at the building's thresholds.

Conceptually, the project is comprised of a series of folded planes working in tandem with chosen materials to achieve proper solar orientation and energy efficiency. A thick rammed-earth wall folds from west to south to east exposures, shielding the interior from the harshest solar gain. The translucent polycarbonate panels fold from the north to the shaded east wall, admitting daylight at the most favorable exposures. Corrugated metal panels fold from the high west wall, over the roof, and down the east wall, reflecting the sun and protecting the large, sliding door panel that opens the living room to the outdoors.

The residence was constructed on an infill lot in a neighborhood within the City of Tucson Empowerment Zone. The adjacent context consists of a large stock of houses built from the 1920s to the 1950s, in generally poor condition, with a few new houses on infill lots. This house accommodates a stable, working family in a distressed area.

This dwelling serves as an energy-conscious prototype for the long, narrow lots with predominantly east-west solar exposure, commonly found in Tucson. It is difficult to control unwanted solar gain when most of the exterior wall and window area faces east and west. Residence One has an eighteen-inch-thick rammed-earth wall along the seventy-six-foot-long west exposure, with no openings for solar gain. The thermal mass of this wall behaves as an energy flywheel, slowly gaining heat during direct sun exposure and re-radiating it into the cool night sky before it can enter the interior of the home. This strategy is particularly well-suited to hot, arid regions.

The south wall and most of the east wall is rammed earth as well, with the protected north wall and east wall, under the carport roof, built as steel frames with operable windows or translucent polycarbonate sheathing. A large, sliding door panel opens the living room up to the carport space, which doubles the public space for the eight months of the year when it is pleasant to live outside in this climate.

The landscape will also participate in the passive solar strategy for minimizing utilities costs in the residence. Deciduous paloverde trees were planted on the south side of the house to shade the rammed-earth wall, and fast-growing eucalypti were planted along the west side to quickly gain shade for that exposure. Two fruit trees—lemon and pomegranate—are planted near the east carport where they will receive roof-water run-off. Agave and ocotillos are used in the front yard where little run-off water is available.

The construction materials were chosen for durability and thermal properties. Rammed earth is sealed and never has to be painted, plastered, or patched. The steel roof and

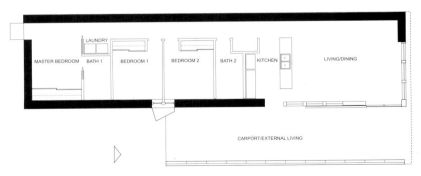

Floor plan

OPPOSITE
Exterior view at night

wall panels have thirty-year waranties, and the steel framing is termite-proof. The polycarbonate panels are more resilient and robust than glass and have a ten year warranty against ultra violet discoloration. Donations from several community partners have helped make this project feasible. A local steel supplier offered an innovative engineering design for the steel framing, and the concrete footings and floor slab were donated by a well established construction company. Except for the concrete floor, plumbing, and mechanical work, all of the construction was done by students and faculty. The xeriscape landscaping was designed by landscape architecture students and implemented by local high school National Honor Society students.

The faculty and students involved in this project designed the methods of construction to reduce the cost of dwelling by avoiding the necessity for heavy equipment, expensive materials, and customized tools. The formwork for the rammed-earth walls, for example, was designed and fabricated of lightweight plywood and dimensional lumber held together with pipe clamps. This armature could be assembled and disassembled quickly by only a few people without lifting equipment, and enabled the reuse of the same pieces multiple times. The formwork was also configured to allow the bond beam to be poured before removing the forms by holding back the concrete the length of the required rebar splice, thus allowing the reinforcing steel to be continuous, even though the concrete was poured in small batches.

TOP: Light gauge steel structure
BOTTOM: Construction

OPPOSITE
TOP: Rammed-earth sequence
BOTTOM: Construction

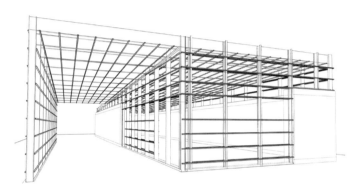

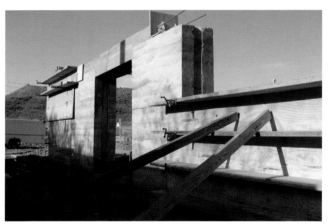

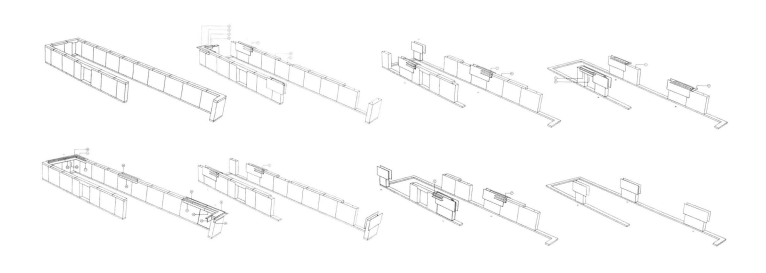

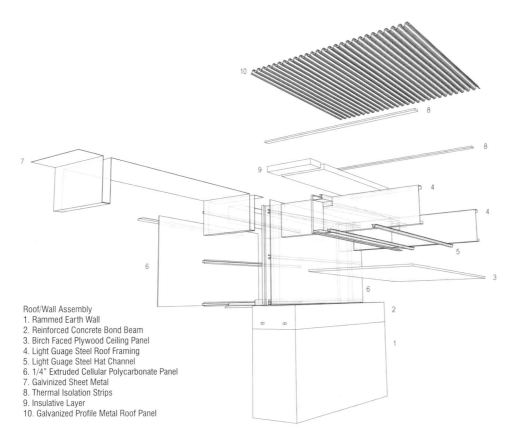

TOP: Exploded construction detail
BOTTOM: Kitchen

OPPOSITE
TOP LEFT: Sliding entry door exterior
TOP RIGHT: Exploded sliding door assembly
BOTTOM: Rammed-earth walls and light-gauge steel framing

Roof/Wall Assembly
1. Rammed Earth Wall
2. Reinforced Concrete Bond Beam
3. Birch Faced Plywood Ceiling Panel
4. Light Guage Steel Roof Framing
5. Light Guage Steel Hat Channel
6. 1/4" Extruded Cellular Polycarbonate Panel
7. Galvinized Sheet Metal
8. Thermal Isolation Strips
9. Insulative Layer
10. Galvanized Profile Metal Roof Panel

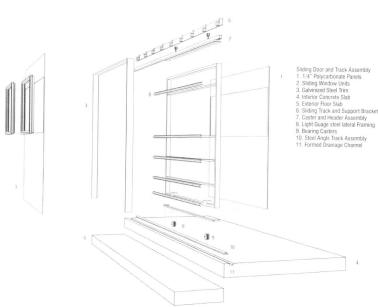

Sliding Door and Track Assembly
1. 1/4" Polycarbonate Panels
2. Sliding Window Units
3. Galvinized Steel Trim
4. Interior Concrete Slab
5. Exterior Floor Slab
6. Sliding Track and Support Bracket
7. Caster and Header Assembly
8. Light Guage steel lateral Framing
9. Bearing Casters
10. Steel Angle Track Assembly
11. Formed Drainage Channel

# ecoMOD

University of Virginia, Charlottesville, Virginia

—————

University of Virginia School of Architecture/John Quale

**PROJECT DIRECTOR:** John Quale
**ENGINEERING DIRECTOR:** Paxton Marshall
**RESEARCH ASSISTANT:** Carolina Shaban
**SCHOOL OF ARCHITECTURE ADVISORS:** Ted Marrs, Abrahamse & Company, Builders; Greg Sloditskie, Modular Building, Advisor; Dr. S. Mujdem Vural, Nisha Botchwey, SARC Community Planning Advisors; Chris Fanin, SARC Lecturer; Julie Bargmann, SARC Associate Professor; Kirk Martini, SARC Structural Engineering Advisor; Robert Cowel
**MECHANICAL ENGINEERING ADVISORS:** Harry Powell, SEAS Computer Systems Engineer; Julie Zimmerman, SEAS Life Cycle Assessment Advisor; Mark White, McIntire School of Commerce Advisor; Other Advisors: Bryan Bell, Chris Benton, Eric Gilchrist, Tom Kavounas, Jeff Saul, John Meggs, Sara Osborne, Roger Rothwell, Roger Rothwell, Jr., Alyson Sappington, Mark Schulyer
**CLIENT:** Stu Armstrong, Executive Director; Mark Watson, Project Development Manager; Peter Loach, Deputy Director of Operations
**ARCH401/ARCH801/LAR801 DESIGN STUDIO, FALL 2004:** Christopher Brooks, Steven Cornell, Barrett Eastwood, Greg Harris, David Hill, Thomas Holloman, Susan Hughes, Marilyn Moedinger, Yvi Nyugen, Ben Patrick, Christina Robinette, Robert Schmidt
**ARCH402/ARCH802/LAR802 DESIGN STUDIO, SPRING 2005:** Christopher Brooks, Page Durrant, Barret Eastwood, Meredith Epley, Lauren Hackney, Greg Harris, David Hill, Thomas Holloman, George Kincaid, Gus Lynch, Marilyn Moedinger, Ben Patrick, Christina Robinette, Garrett Rouzer, Casey Servis, Carolina Shaban, Kyle Sturgeon, Lacey Wolf
**ENGR 499 BUILDING ENERGY SYSTEMS DESIGN AND EVALUATION, SPRING 2005:** Alex Arsenovic, Godwin Nestor, Jeff Rominger, Kyle Yetter
**ECOMOD1 BUILD TEAM SUMMER/FALL 2005:** Galin Boyd, Christopher Brooks, Pager Durant, Barrett Eastwood, Meredith Eply, Lauren Hackney, Thomas Holloman, George Kincaid, Gus Lynch, Marilyn Moedinger, Garret Rouzer, Casey Servis, Carolina Shaban, Kyle Sturgeon; volunteers: Matthew Clay, Trevor Taub, Julie Bargmann, Heidi Baker, Laura Bandera, Corey Barnes, Anne Bohlen, Neil Bidzinski, Mark Buenavista, Nathan Cunningham, Doug Daley, Brian Duffy, Stephan Dunstan, Ken Eastwood, Bonnye Eastwood, Carmen Fanzone, Whit Faulconer, Sarah Foster, Lauren Fracescone, David Gardner, Mike Goldin, Brittany Gjormand, Mark Holmquist, Amy Lewandowski, Matthew Machaj, Catherine Manza, Kathleen Mark, JP Mays, Linn Moedinger, Susan Moedinger, David Mullen, Daniel Norman, Sarah Oehl, Jordan Phemister, James Pressley, Sarah Scruggs, Elizabeth Shoffner, Catherine Manza, Courtney Spearman, Amanda Taylor, Elaine Uang, Justin Walton, Michael Wenrich, Bret White

**ARCH 530 EVALUATING ECOMOD, FALL 2005:** Christina Calabrese, Leyland del Re, Chris Dunn, Whit Faulconer, Mark Holmquist, Anand Kanoria, Andy Klepic, Amelia McKeithen, Greta Modesitt, Melinda Sathre, Lauren Shirley, Betul Tuncer, Elaine Uang
**ARCH 536 EVALUATING ECOMOD, SPRING 2006:** Christina Calabrese, Patrica Vaz De Carvalho, Adam Donovan, Sally Foster, Mark Holmquist, Elizabeth Kahley, Chad Logan, JP Mays, Molly O'Donnell, Rosalyn Schmitt, Carol Shiflett, Lauren Shirley, Matthew Young, Toby Zhang
**ENGR 495 BUILDING ENERGY SYSTEMS DESIGN AND EVALUATION, FALL 2005:** Tristan Becker, Sarah Foster, Scottie Gambill, Benjamin Kidd, Alex McCarthy, Joshua Palmer, Alison Tramba, Debora Wesner, Brooke Yamakoshi, Caroline Zennie
**ENGR 499 BUILDING ENERGY SYSTEMS DESIGN AND EVALUATION, SPRING 2006:** Tristan Becker, Sarah Foster, Scottie Gambill, Ping Guan, Benjamin Kidd, Michael Lewis, Alex McCarthy, Joshua Palmer, Alison Tramba, Debra Wesner, Brooke Yamakoshi, Caroline Zennie

The ecoMOD project at the University of Virginia School of Architecture has developed a series of prefabricated, affordable, and ecological housing types under the direction of Assistant Professor John Quale. The focus here, ecoMOD1, was completed for the Piedmont Housing Alliance in Charlottesville, Virginia. The ecoMOD2 was completed in Gautier, Mississippi, for Habitat for Humanity in the summer of 2007. The ecoMOD3 was fabricated in Charlottesville, Virginia, in 2007 for the Piedmont Housing

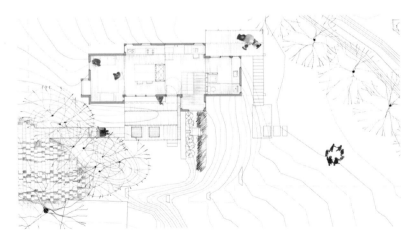

Site plan and ground floor

OPPOSITE
TOP: Kitchen
BOTTOM: Front deck

Alliance. A fourth house is planned and will be researched, designed, built, and evaluated by 2010. Each of the projects are integrated at the level of the curriculum, the community, and the house.

Students from several adjacent disciplines (architecture, engineering, landscape architecture, historic preservation, business, environmental science, planning, and economics) participate in the research, design, construction, and evaluation of each housing type. The project and students also benefit from outside professional advisors on issues critical to each housing type. This introduces students to the benefits of integrated design at the undergraduate and graduate levels. The student exposure to construction, energy modeling, and nonprofit work cannot be underestimated. Emerging from a broad social justice agenda and a pedagogical desire to provide instruction through construction, the project yields housing for people who often cannot afford such housing, much less the energy to operate them.

The first of four ecoMOD projects, ecoMOD1, utilizes eight prefabricated modules fabricated with structural insulated panels (SIPs) in an off-site, University owned airplane hanger. The SIPs panels provide a highly energy-efficient building envelope that minimizes the waste stream encountered in construction. The house has a stormwater harvesting system that yields potable water from roof-collected water. Roof water is collected in 3,400-gallon tanks below the entry deck. The water passes through a series of carbon and ultra violet filters before it is potable. Solar hot water panels provide domestic hot water. A primary goal was to reduce the residents' utility bills by

two-thirds. Also known as the OUTin House, the design program includes the entire lot, and much of the house's life is envisioned outside. The configuration of the modules and apertures maximize interaction among interior and exterior spaces. On the exterior, drought-tolerant plants and water-retention strategies point toward more productive residential landscapes.

A key aspect of the project is the evaluation of each house to verify the claims embedded in design decisions. Many claims about energy and material efficiency are frequently made, especially in the residential market, but are rarely quantified or verified. Data from the ecoMOD will serve as a benchmark for housing in the coming years. Throughout the house, ecoMOD1 has monitoring systems and sensors that provide daily data on energy and water consumption, indoor air quality, and interior and exterior temperatures. The energy performance of the house and its systems is currently being evaluated through several graduate students' theses. An embodied energy comparison of a prefabricated house and the same house constructed on-site is also currently under evaluation. Postoccupancy evaluations of the residents document other aspects of the house's performance.

The project has numerous lessons that apply in other contexts as well. The argument for modular construction here focuses on quality control, material efficiencies, and speed of on-site assembly. The project challenges the residential construction industry to adopt more integrated practices with reliable data and statistics based upon the performance of the ecoMOD projects.

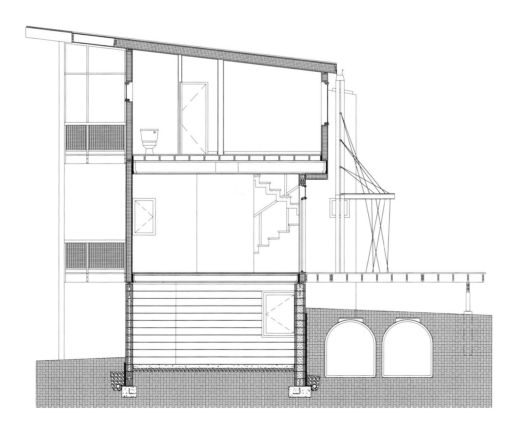

Section at kitchen

OPPOSITE
TOP: Upper level plan
CENTER: Main level plan
BOTTOM: Lower level plan

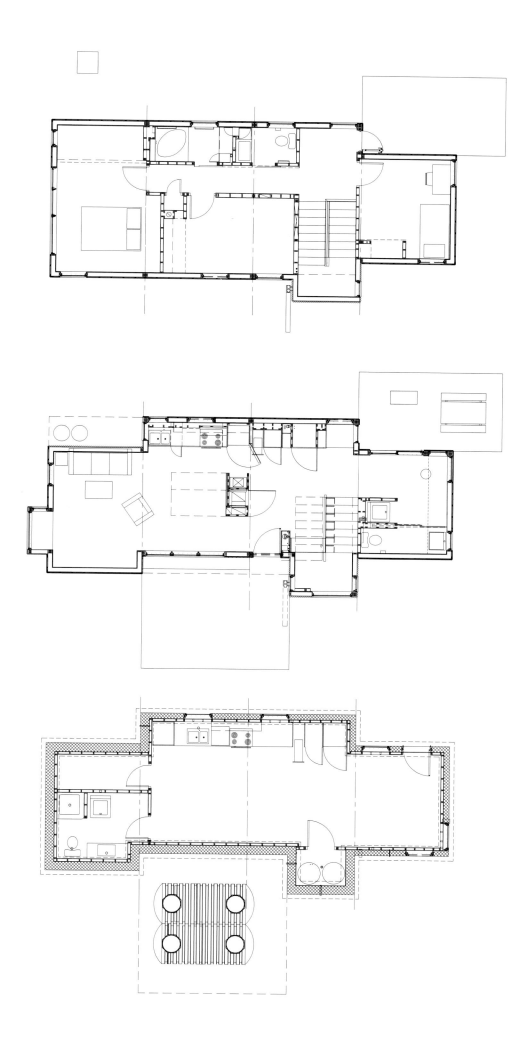

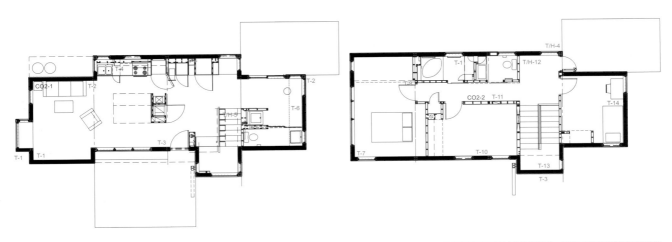

1
2
3
4
5
6
7
8

TOP: Living room view
MIDDLE: Bedroom with solar control
BOTTOM: Kitchen transformation

OPPOSITE
TOP: Stair views
BOTTOM LEFT: Box window
BOTTOM RIGHT: Water collection downspout

# Chicago Residence

Chicago, Illinois

―――――

Wheeler Kearns Architects, Chicago, Illinois

ARCHITECT: Wheeler Kearns Architects, with Xavier Vendrell Studio
STRUCTURAL ENGINEERING: Thornton Tomasetti
MEP/GEOTHERMAL ENGINEERING: IBC Engineering
LANDSCAPE ARCHITECT: McKay Landscape Architects
CIVIL ENGINEERING: V3 Consultants
LIGHTING: Charter Sills & Associates
ACOUSTICAL ENGINEERING: Acoustic Expertise
GENERAL CONTRACTOR: NORCON
GLAZING SYSTEMS: James Carpenter Design Associates
INTERIOR FURNISHINGS: Leslie Jones and Associates
WINDOW WASHING: Donald Hamel Window Cleaning Co.
SECURITY: Titan Security
CONTROLS: Control Engineering
AUDIO-VISUAL: Baumeister Electronic Architects
OWNERS' REPRESENTATIVE: Project Management Advisors

The Chicago Residence is a house for a family of four on five contiguous parcels in Lincoln Park. The brief called for an intimately scaled environment for family activities that could be transformed into an assembly space for ninety people. The caliber of the art collection and a desire for durability called for museum-quality standards. An integral connection between interior and exterior experiences was also required. A scheme of contrasts was developed where the contained, introverted private functions of the house float above the expansive, extroverted public functions at grade. A series of open voids punctuate and interconnect the composition of the house, containing reflecting pools, private courts, and overlooks; each moving light and air through the section.

To maximize the desired transparency at grade, the private zone of the house cantilevers forty feet over the ground floor. To achieve this cantilever, the second story is a vertically and horizontally posttensioned concrete box structure with twelve-inch slabs and eight-inch walls that bear upon the sixteen-inch-thick stair-tower walls, which in turn bear on caissons that extend one hundred feet down to bedrock. Vertical posttensioned cables are anchored thirty-five feet into the bedrock. To control long-term deflection, eight 2.5-inch and eight 1.75-inch-diameter steel posttensioned threaded rods were situated on the north side of the house, some exposed to view. To control long-term concrete creep, five one-inch finger-jointed solid steel plates (forty-eight inches deep and the height of the building) were embedded in the stair walls. Wheeler Kearns worked with Joseph Burns of Thornton Tomasetti on the structural strategy with Werner Sobek as the City of Chicago's peer-review engineer.

The private zone is superinsulated, offsetting thermal losses on the glazed ground floor—in essence a building wearing a "parka and shorts." To minimize thermal conductivity, the concrete box was clad with a series of four-inch pultruded fiberglass sections, filled with closed cell-spray insulation. Three-inch-thick aerated-autoclaved concrete panels were attached to the fiberglass sections as an insulating lightweight substrate for a cement stucco finish. The interior of the concrete was directly plastered, allowing the structure to act as a thermal sink. The seventeen-inch-deep wall assembly has deep punched apertures for the introverted private zone. Southern glazing is protected by overhangs and localized planting. All roofs are superinsulated and incorporate either extensive or

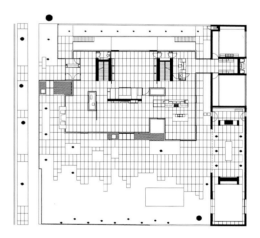

TOP: Ground floor
BOTTOM: Second floor
OPPOSITE
Exterior view

72

intensive vegetated roof systems. The building uses thirty-five, one hundred-foot-deep geothermal wells as the energy source for hydronic radiant heating and low-velocity cooling throughout the house. Fresh air is taken from the northern courtyard and ducted or tempered through the ground prior to reaching an internal heat exchanger. The energy strategy was developed with Lev Zyenvach of IBC Engineers.

The ground-floor glazing was designed to maximize transparency while minimizing heat loss and damaging ultra violet infiltration. The glass assembly consists of 1.25-inch laminated Starphire (low-iron), insulated, structurally sealed units. The glass units work in concert with T-shaped bronze mullions, located on the warm side, which in turn support the top-hung sliding doors, each weighing up to 1,100 pounds. The doors and jamb liners are thermally broken. This glazing assembly is the product of structural, thermal, light, visual, and acoustic optimization. Exterior grills cover the perimeter trench drain, which mirrors the interior air-diffuser grill. This solution allows is a seamless, flush transition of the brush-honed limestone floor, set on a four-foot seven-inch grid, from the interior to the gardens. Wheeler Kearns Architects consulted with James Carpenter Design Associates on the glazing assemblies.

Given the unique nature of the design, the entire first floor of the house was mocked up during the design process in an empty office space to educate the client on the scale and proportion of the space, as well as to conduct lighting and acoustic studies. These studies led to the first floors' warm Douglas fir ceiling slats, which are profiled to direct sound into acoustic insulation above. Glass-beaded BASWAphon was integrated where an acoustically absorptive plaster-like ceiling was required.

Given the nature of living in a "glass house in the city," the client required privacy from the street while affording the public a view to the extensive gardens. An alternating, dynamic bronze-bladed six-foot-high fence was designed with Xavier Vendrell Studio, strategically designed to allow selected discrete views of the garden, while screening views into the house.

The project was the product of close collaboration between an inspired client and a design team assembled at the outset of the project, which grew to a list of fourteen firms of specific expertise working in concert with the negotiated construction team. The photographs illustrate the house as it nears completion.

Section drawing

OPPOSITE
Southeast corner views

Concrete structure and diagrams

OPPOSITE
TOP: Building envelope assembly ground floor
BOTTOM: Before and after at entry

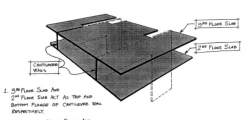

1. 3ʳᵈ FLOOR SLAB AND 2ⁿᵈ FLOOR SLAB ACT AS TOP AND BOTTOM FLANGE OF CANTILEVER WALL RESPECTIVELY.
2. 3ʳᵈ AND 2ⁿᵈ FLOOR SLABS ARE SUPPORTED BY EXTERIOR WALL AND CANTILEVER WALLS

CONCRETE SLAB

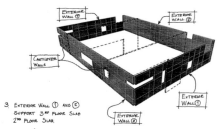

3. EXTERIOR WALL ① AND ② SUPPORT 3ʳᵈ FLOOR SLAB 2ⁿᵈ FLOOR SLAB.
4. EXTERIOR WALL ① IS SUPPORTED BY EXTERIOR WALL ② AND EXTERIOR WALL ② IS SUPPORTED BY CANTILEVER WALLS

PERIMETER CONCRETE WALL

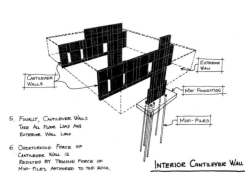

5. FINALLY, CANTILEVER WALLS TAKE ALL FLOOR LOAD AND EXTERIOR WALL LOAD.
6. OVERTURNING FORCE OF CANTILEVER WALL IS RESISTED BY TENSION FORCE OF MINI-PILES ANCHORED TO THE ROCK.

INTERIOR CANTILEVER WALL

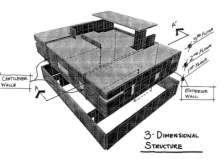

3-DIMENSIONAL STRUCTURE

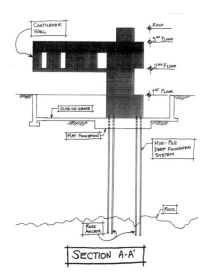

SECTION A-A'

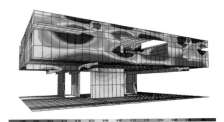

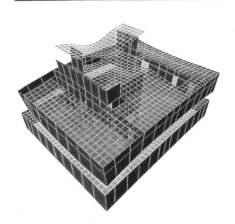

Light shaft and stair

OPPOSITE
Building envelope assembly

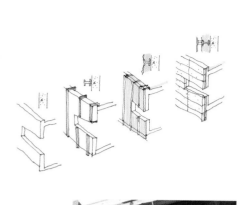

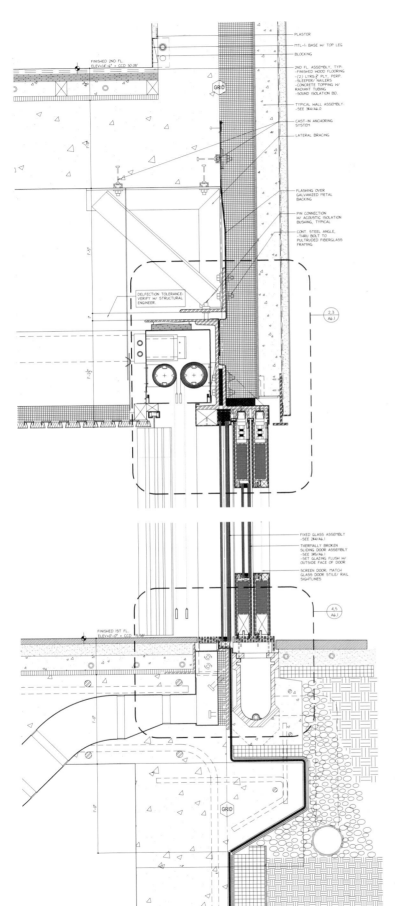

PLASTER

MTL-I: BASE W/ TOP LEG

BLOCKING

2ND FL. ASSEMBLY, TYP.:
-FINISHED WOOD FLOORING
-(2) LYRS-¾" PLT, PERP.
-SLEEPER/ NAILERS
-CONCRETE TOPPING W/
 RADIANT TUBING
-SOUND ISOLATION BD.

TYPICAL WALL ASSEMBLY:
-SEE 3&4/A6.0

CAST-IN ANCHORING
SYSTEM

LATERAL BRACING

FLASHING OVER
GALVANIZED METAL
BACKING

PIN CONNECTION
W/ ACOUSTIC ISOLATION
BUSHING, TYPICAL

CONT. STEEL ANGLE,
-THRU BOLT TO
PULTRUDED FIBERGLASS
FRAMING

FINISHED 2ND FL.
ELEV.+14'-6" +/- CCD 30.08'

GRID

DEFLECTION TOLERANCE:
VERIFY W/ STRUCTURAL
ENGINEER.

2,3
A6.1

FIXED GLASS ASSEMBLY
-SEE 2&4/A6.1

THERMALLY BROKEN
SLIDING DOOR ASSEMBLY
-SEE 3&5/A6.1
-SET GLAZING FLUSH W/
 OUTSIDE FACE OF DOOR

SCREEN DOOR; MATCH
GLASS DOOR STILE/ RAIL
SIGHTLINES

4,5
A6.1

FINISHED 1ST FL.
ELEV.+0'-0" +/- CCD 15.58'

GRID

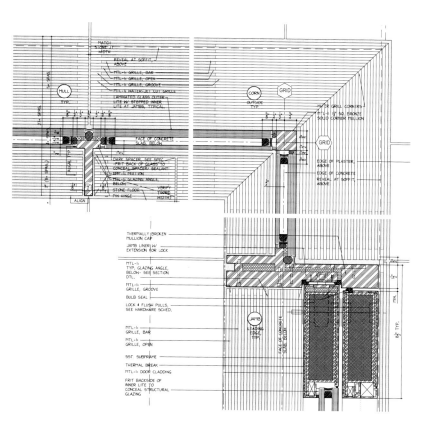

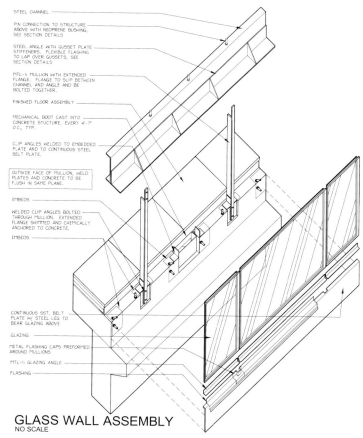

**GLASS WALL ASSEMBLY**
NO SCALE

# New Residence at the Swiss Embassy

Washington, D.C.

Steven Holl Architects, New York City, New York; Rüssli Architekten, Lucerne, Switzerland

**ARCHITECTS:** Steven Holl Architects, Rüssli Architekten AG: Steven Holl and Justin Rüssli, Design Architects; Olaf Schmidt, Stephen O'Dell, Project Architects SHA; Arnault Biou, Peter Englaender, Annette Goderbauer, Li Hu, Irene Vogt, Project Team SHA; Mimi Kueh, Project Architect RA; Andreas Gervasi, Phillip Röösli, Rafael Schnyder, Urs Zuercher, Project Team RA
**STRUCTURAL ENGINEERS:** AF Steffen Engineers (Luzern), Robert Silman Associates (Washington, D.C.)
**MECHANICAL ENGINEERS:** B+B Energietechnik AG (Gisikon), B2E Consulting Engineers (Leesburg, Virginia)
**LANDSCAPE ARCHITECT:** Robert Gissinger (Luzern)
**GENERAL CONTRACTOR:** James G. Davis Construction (Rockville, Maryland), Niersberger Gebäudetecnik (Pforzheim)
**CLIENT:** Swiss Federal Office for Building and Logistics
**INTERIOR DESIGNER:** Hannes Wettstein (Zurich)

The New Residence at the Swiss Embassy is the official residence of the Swiss ambassador to the United States. The project was collaboratively designed and won by Steven Holl and previous collaborator Justin Rüssli through an anonymous competition. The building serves as an ambassadorial residence, but also contains embassy work space and space for formal dining receptions and gallery functions. The first floor of the building contains the more public functions, while the private spaces of the residence are on the second floor. Sited on a hill in Northwest Washington, D.C., the building is organized so a view of the Washington Monument is framed by the legs of the Swiss cruciform plan. The legs of the cruciform plan also frame the entrance, reflecting pools, an herb garden, and other exterior gathering spaces.

The building meets the Swiss MINERGIE energy standard for European buildings. To achieve this energy standard, the building uses highly insulated wall and glazing assemblies, hydronic heating and cooling integrated in the building's concrete structure, a vegetated roof, solar-control devices, and highly efficient mechanical systems from Central Europe. The south-facing orientations are configured to maximize passive-solar control. A building management system controls the operation of the sunshades. A vegetated roof is important to the thermal envelope of the building as extra insulation and a cool roof in the summer. The vegetated roof also helps mitigate stormwater events. Renewable bamboo floors and terrazzo floors containing recycled glass were used.

The building is a fine example of the maximal within the minimal. The approach to the building envelope achieves maximal visual and architectural effects while consuming minimal energy. The board-formed concrete structure is tinted with integral dark-charcoal pigments. The sandblasted glass channels form a rain screen in front of a white waterproof membrane. The aim of these two systems is to recall the dark stone and white snow of the Swiss Alps. The translucent rain screen and translucent or transparent apertures engender a range of readings and are essential to the solar-control strategy for the building. Translucent/opaque, translucent/transparent, sun-screen veiled transparent, and transparent textures merge both aesthetic and performance agendas. The channel glass is spaced in front of the white thermal envelope and exterior rigid insulation. A gap at the base of the channel glass and a vent on the backside of the stainless steel coping vents the rain-screen cavity at the top of the wall. Here, Holl's sustained interest in phenomenological performances begins to merge with certain energy performances. In this case, aspects of the architectural intent are inexplicably intertwined with performative intentions. In the strongest examples of integrated design, architectural intentions will anticipate, engender, and amplify the roles of construction and energy consistently throughout the design process.

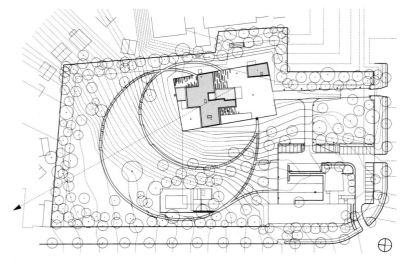

Site plan with view to Washington Monument

OPPOSITE
TOP: Day
BOTTOM: Evening

TOP: South and east
elevations
BOTTOM: Oblique view
from landscape

OPPOSITE
TOP: Ground floor plan
BOTTOM: Exterior

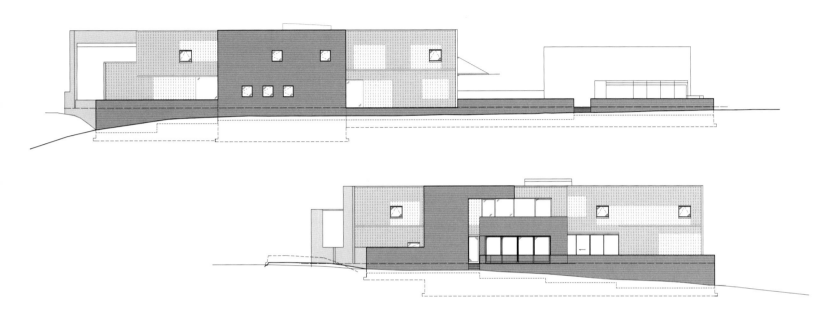

84

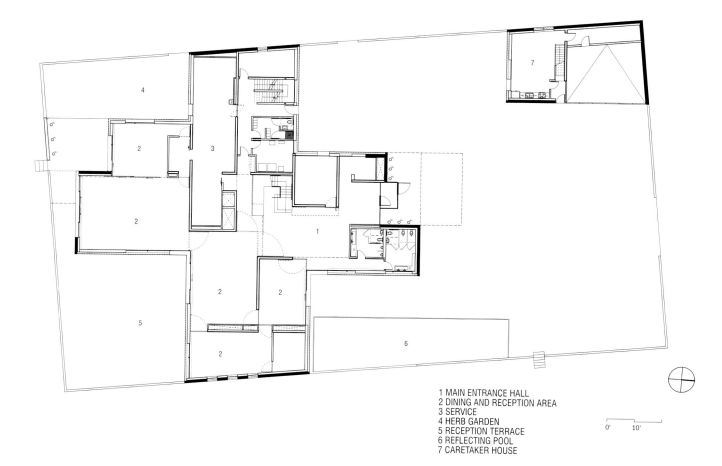

1 MAIN ENTRANCE HALL
2 DINING AND RECEPTION AREA
3 SERVICE
4 HERB GARDEN
5 RECEPTION TERRACE
6 REFLECTING POOL
7 CARETAKER HOUSE

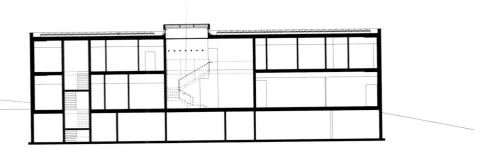

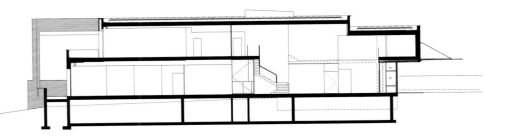

TOP: Sections
BOTTOM: Interior View

OPPOSITE
TOP: Glass channel wall
assembly
MIDDLE: Glass channel
plan detail
BOTTOM: Glass channel
wall view

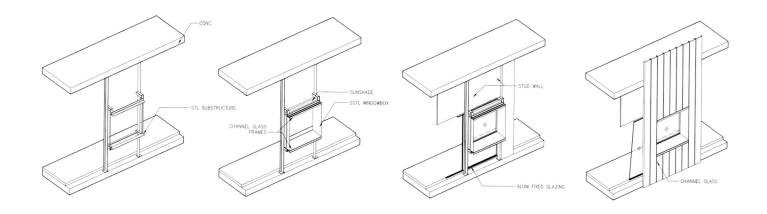

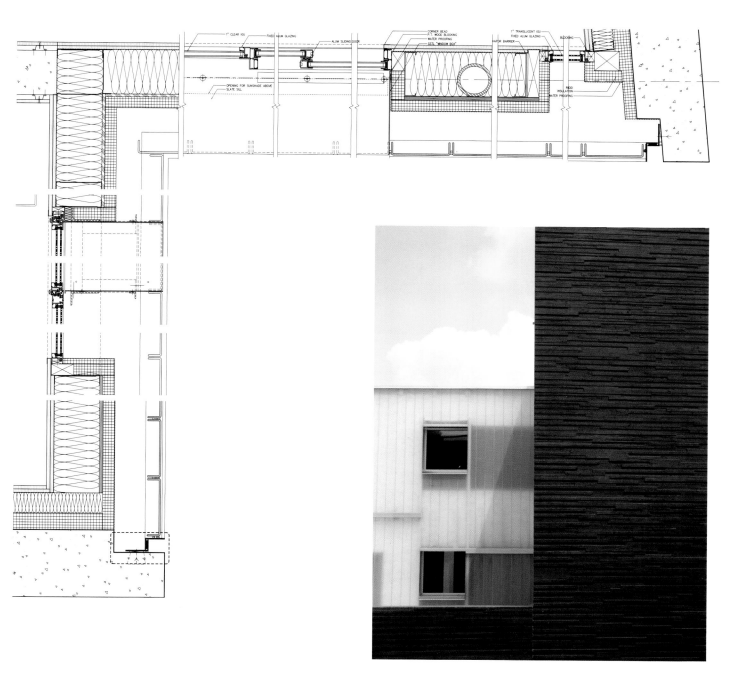

87

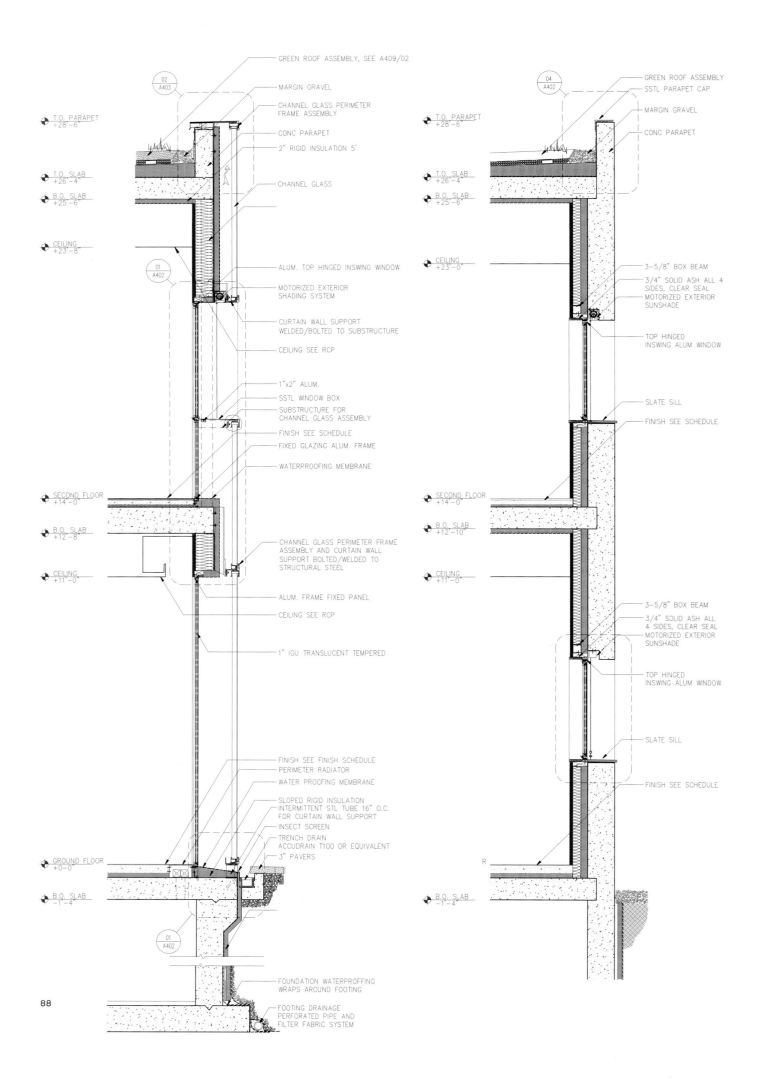

GREEN ROOF ASSEMBLY, SEE A409/02

MARGIN GRAVEL

CHANNEL GLASS PERIMETER FRAME ASSEMBLY

CONC PARAPET

2" RIGID INSULATION 5'

CHANNEL GLASS

ALUM. TOP HINGED INSWING WINDOW

MOTORIZED EXTERIOR SHADING SYSTEM

CURTAIN WALL SUPPORT WELDED/BOLTED TO SUBSTRUCTURE

CEILING SEE RCP

1"x2" ALUM.

SSTL WINDOW BOX

SUBSTRUCTURE FOR CHANNEL GLASS ASSEMBLY

FINISH SEE SCHEDULE

FIXED GLAZING ALUM. FRAME

WATERPROOFING MEMBRANE

CHANNEL GLASS PERIMETER FRAME ASSEMBLY AND CURTAIN WALL SUPPORT BOLTED/WELDED TO STRUCTURAL STEEL

ALUM. FRAME FIXED PANEL

CEILING SEE RCP

1" IGU TRANSLUCENT TEMPERED

FINISH SEE FINISH SCHEDULE

PERIMETER RADIATOR

WATER PROOFING MEMBRANE

SLOPED RIGID INSULATION INTERMITTENT STL TUBE 16" O.C. FOR CURTAIN WALL SUPPORT

INSECT SCREEN

TRENCH DRAIN ACCUDRAIN T100 OR EQUIVALENT

3" PAVERS

FOUNDATION WATERPROFFING WRAPS AROUND FOOTING

FOOTING DRAINAGE PERFORATED PIPE AND FILTER FABRIC SYSTEM

T.O. PARAPET +28'-6"

T.O. SLAB +26'-4"

B.O. SLAB +25'-6"

CEILING +23'-8"

SECOND FLOOR +14'-0"

B.O. SLAB +12'-8"

CEILING +11'-0"

GROUND FLOOR +0'-0"

B.O. SLAB -1'-4"

02 A403

01 A402

01 A402

GREEN ROOF ASSEMBLY

SSTL PARAPET CAP

MARGIN GRAVEL

CONC PARAPET

3-5/8" BOX BEAM

3/4" SOLID ASH ALL 4 SIDES, CLEAR SEAL

MOTORIZED EXTERIOR SUNSHADE

TOP HINGED INSWING ALUM WINDOW

SLATE SILL

FINISH SEE SCHEDULE

3-5/8" BOX BEAM

3/4" SOLID ASH ALL 4 SIDES, CLEAR SEAL

MOTORIZED EXTERIOR SUNSHADE

TOP HINGED INSWING ALUM WINDOW

SLATE SILL

FINISH SEE SCHEDULE

T.O. PARAPET +28'-6"

T.O. SLAB +26'-4"

B.O. SLAB +25'-6"

CEILING +23'-0"

SECOND FLOOR +14'-0"

B.O. SLAB +12'-10"

CEILING +11'-0"

B.O. SLAB -1'-4"

04 A402

R

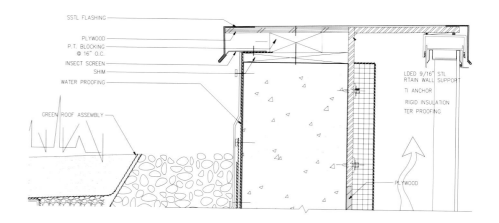

SSTL FLASHING
PLYWOOD
P.T. BLOCKING @ 16" O.C.
INSECT SCREEN
SHIM
WATER PROOFING

GREEN ROOF ASSEMBLY

LDED 9/16" STL RTAIN WALL SUPPORT
TI ANCHOR
RIGID INSULATION
TER PROOFING

PLYWOOD

Glass channel details

OPPOSITE
LEFT: Channel glass wall section
RIGHT: Concrete wall section

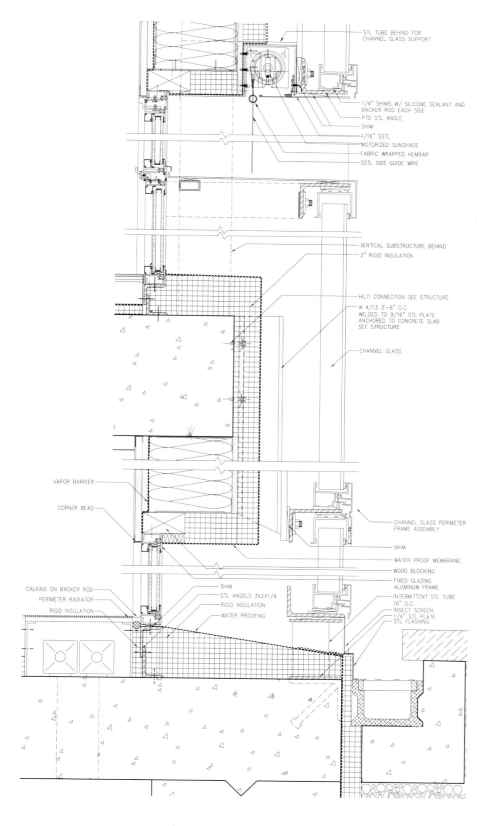

STL TUBE BEHIND FOR CHANNEL GLASS SUPPORT

1/4" SHIMS W/ SILICONE SEALANT AND BACKER ROD EACH SIDE
PTD STL ANGLE
SHIM
1/16" SSTL
MOTORIZED SUNSHADE
FABRIC WRAPPED HEMBAR
SSTL SIDE GUIDE WIRE

VERTICAL SUBSTRUCTURE BEHIND
2" RIGID INSULATION

HILTI CONNECTION SEE STRUCTURE

W 4/13 3'-6" O.C.
WELDED TO 9/16" STL PLATE ANCHORED TO CONCRETE SLAB SEE STRUCTURE

CHANNEL GLASS

VAPOR BARRIER

CORNER BEAD

CHANNEL GLASS PERIMETER FRAME ASSEMBLY

SHIM
WATER PROOF MEMBRANE
WOOD BLOCKING
FIXED GLAZING ALUMINUM FRAME

CALKING ON BACKER ROD
PERIMETER RADIATOR
RIGID INSULATION

SHIM
STL ANGELS 3X2X1/4
RIGID INSULATION
WATER PROOFING

INTERMITTENT STL TUBE 16" O.C.
INSECT SCREEN
1/4" STL PLATE
STL FLASHING

89

# Museum of Contemporary Art

Denver, Colorado

Adjaye Associates, London, England

**DESIGN ARCHITECT:** Adjaye Associates
David Adjaye, Principal; Joe Franchina, Project Director
**ARCHITECT OF RECORD:** Davis Partnership Architects
Brit Probst, Principal-in-Charge; Maria Cole, Architect;
Eric Crotty, Landscape Architect
**STRUCTURAL ENGINEER:** Martin/Martin
**MECHANICAL, ELECTRICAL, SECURITY, AND TELECOM:**
M-E Engineers
**CIVIL ENGINEER:** MB Consulting
**LIGHTING CONSULTANT:** Hefferan Partnership Lighting
Design
**GENERAL CONTRACTOR:** M. A. Mortenson
**FIRE PROTECTION AND LIFE SAFETY:** Rolf Jensen &
Associates, Inc.
**ENERGY MODELING CONSULTANT:** Enermodal Engineering
**FACADE ENGINEER:** Dewhurst Macfarlane and Partners

Adjaye Associates won the commission for the 25,000-square-foot Museum of Contemporary Art in Denver, Colorado. The new facility contains gallery space, education space, lecture space, a book store, and a roof garden. In welcome contrast to other recent museums, the Museum of Contemporary Art insisted upon "a design that supports rather than defines the Museum's mission." Mirroring its focus on cultural innovations and energy, the architects also sought a design that would be equally cognizant of potential operational innovations and energy. It is located in the rapidly redeveloping South Platte River area just north of downtown Denver. The four-story steel framed structure maintains the height of adjacent residential construction while distinguishing itself through its material palette. The building's rooftop garden is accessible and will provide excellent views of downtown Denver and the Rocky Mountains beyond to the west.

Since the museum has no permanent collection, a range of galleries, each a distinct orthogonal spatial volume, anticipates the spectrum of temporary art installations and exhibits that might occur in the Museum. Not unlike the European *kunsthal* approach, the galleries will focus on specific media such as photography, large works, paper, and digital media. Each gallery will have surfaces, proportions, and lighting appropriate to each medium. The large works gallery will be served by a large door to the loading area and will be supported by additional structures to accommodate heavy work. The design also strategically aims to integrate future unknown content by receding in a limited palette of hues and textures. The building actively supports its program best as a quiet background and receptacle. The primary surfaces are concrete slabs,

white walls, and its unique curtain wall system that will yield a soft diffuse light.

Light is the primary parameter that helped determine the building's morphology. A series of skylights punctuates the interior circulation volumes, which separate and connect the various galleries. The building envelope consists of double glazed units. The outer pane is tinted gray and the inner pane is clear. Both inner faces of the glazing are sandblasted. Within the glazing unit, MonoPan is used to increase the thermal and acoustic insulation value of the assembly while also diffusing light. MonoPan is a proprietary product of ultra violet-stable polypropylene honeycombs that are thermally welded to fiberglass-reinforced polypropylene face sheets. The result will be a milky diffuse quality of light for the galleries and increased thermal performance for the building envelope. Two glass panes above the entrance on the southeast corner will be transparent, offering views of downtown Denver and views into the gallery from the street.

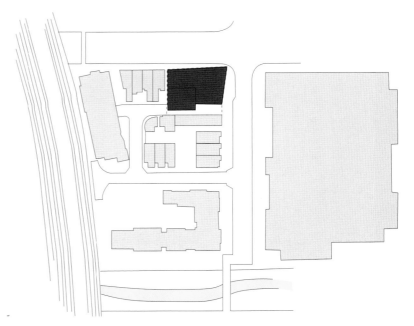

Site plan

OPPOSITE
TOP: Section
BOTTOM: Exterior rendering

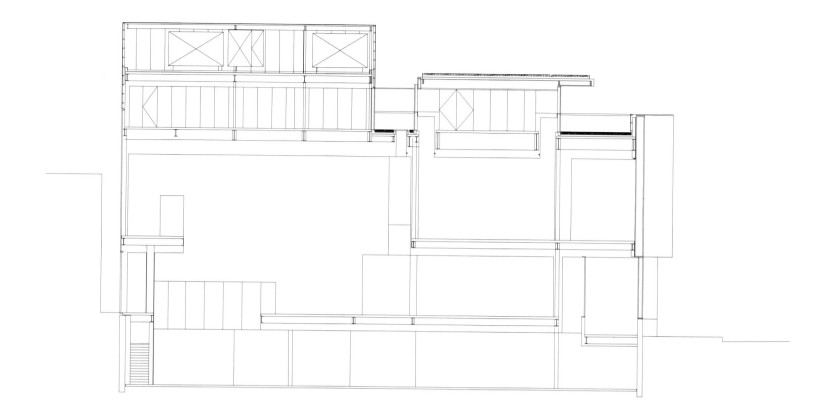

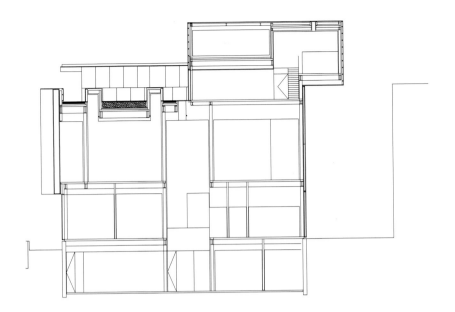

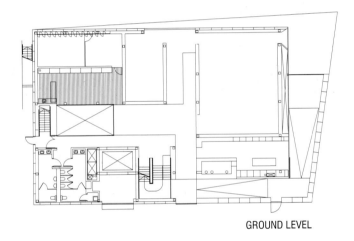

GROUND LEVEL

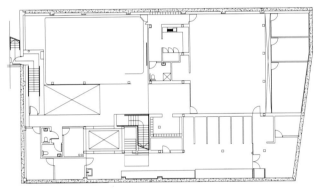

LOWER LEVEL

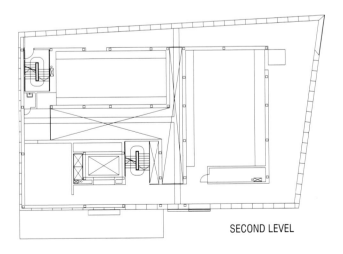

SECOND LEVEL

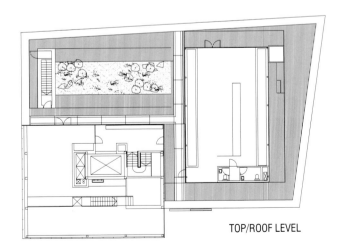

TOP/ROOF LEVEL

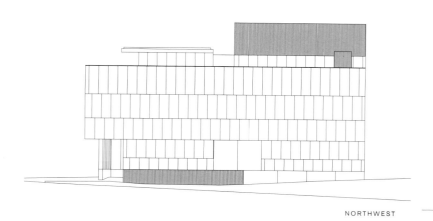

NORTHWEST

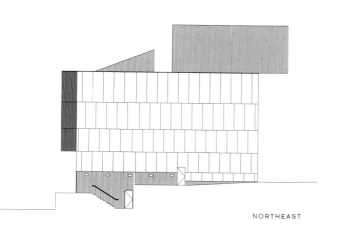

NORTHEAST

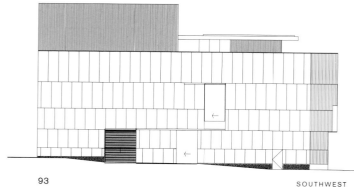

SOUTHWEST

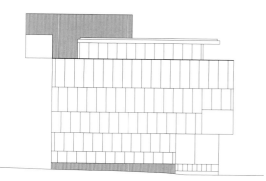

SOUTHEAST

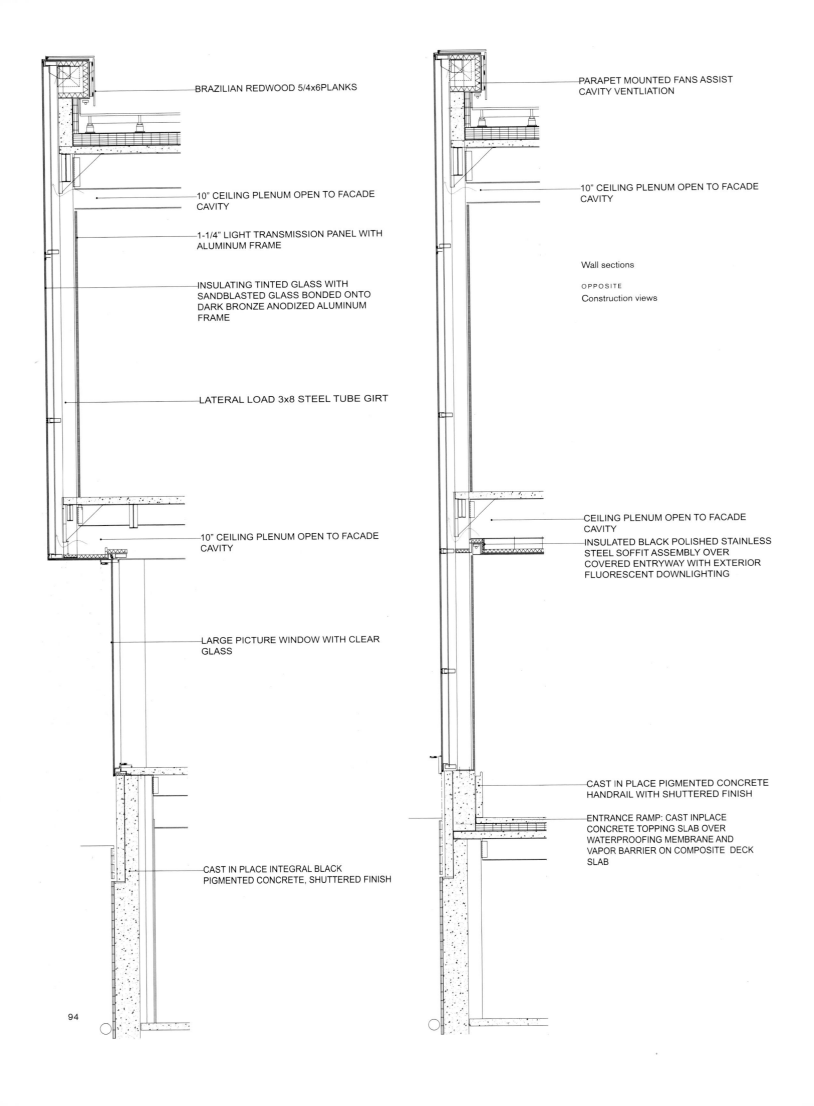

BRAZILIAN REDWOOD 5/4x6PLANKS

10" CEILING PLENUM OPEN TO FACADE CAVITY

1-1/4" LIGHT TRANSMISSION PANEL WITH ALUMINUM FRAME

INSULATING TINTED GLASS WITH SANDBLASTED GLASS BONDED ONTO DARK BRONZE ANODIZED ALUMINUM FRAME

LATERAL LOAD 3x8 STEEL TUBE GIRT

10" CEILING PLENUM OPEN TO FACADE CAVITY

LARGE PICTURE WINDOW WITH CLEAR GLASS

CAST IN PLACE INTEGRAL BLACK PIGMENTED CONCRETE, SHUTTERED FINISH

PARAPET MOUNTED FANS ASSIST CAVITY VENTLIATION

10" CEILING PLENUM OPEN TO FACADE CAVITY

Wall sections

OPPOSITE
Construction views

CEILING PLENUM OPEN TO FACADE CAVITY

INSULATED BLACK POLISHED STAINLESS STEEL SOFFIT ASSEMBLY OVER COVERED ENTRYWAY WITH EXTERIOR FLUORESCENT DOWNLIGHTING

CAST IN PLACE PIGMENTED CONCRETE HANDRAIL WITH SHUTTERED FINISH

ENTRANCE RAMP: CAST INPLACE CONCRETE TOPPING SLAB OVER WATERPROOFING MEMBRANE AND VAPOR BARRIER ON COMPOSITE DECK SLAB

# North Carolina Museum of Art

Raleigh, North Carolina

Thomas Phifer and Partners, New York, New York

DESIGN ARCHITECT: Thomas Phifer and Partners
Thomas Phifer, Principal; Greg Reaves, Project Partner;
Gabriel Smith, Project Architect; Christoph Timm, Adam
Ruffin, Katie Bennett, Kerim Demirkan, Len Lopate,
Jon Benner, Joseph Sevene, Daniel Taft, Eric Richey,
Design Team
EXECUTIVE ARCHITECT: Pearce Brinkley Cease + Lee
Architects, Raleigh, North Carolina: Jeffrey Lee, Clymer
Cease, Principals; David Francis, Project Architect;
Matt Konar, Juliette Dolle, Henry Newell, David Lehman,
Design Team
STRUCTURAL ENGINEERS: Lasater-Hopkins-Chang,
Raleigh, North Carolina; Skidmore, Owings & Merrill
MECHANICAL ENGINEERS: Stanford White; Altieri Sebor
Weiber
LANDSCAPE ARCHITECTS: Peter Walker and Partners,
Berkeley, California: Peter Walker, Principal; Sarah Kuehl,
Project Partner; Daphne Edwards, Michael Oser, Paul
Sieron, Michael Dellis, Design Team
CIVIL ENGINEERS: Kimley-Horn and Associates; ArtifexED
ELECTRIC LIGHTING: Fisher Marantz Stone, New York, New
York: Paul Marantz, Principal
DAYLIGHT ENGINEERING: Arup, London, UK and New York,
New York: Andy Sedgwick, Project Principal
ACOUSTICS: Creative Acoustics, Westport, Connecticut
CONSTRUCTION MANAGEMENT: Barnhill/Centex Contracting
and Construction
OWNER: State of North Carolina: The Honorable Michael F.
Easley, Governor; Lisbeth C. Evans, Secretary, Department
of Cultural Resources
MUSEUM: North Carolina Museum of Art, Raleigh: Dr.
Lawrence J. Wheeler, Director; Daniel P. Gottlieb, Deputy
Director of Planning and Design
LANDSCAPE RENDERINGS: Christopher Grubbs, Illustrator
EXECUTIVE LANDSCAPE ARCHITECTS: Lappas + Havener:
Walter R. Havener, Principal; Jesse Turner, Landscape
Designer
SECURITY: Risk Management Associates; James J. Davis
and Associates
FOOD SERVICE: William Caruso & Associates

The 127,000-square-foot North Carolina Museum of Art expansion project by Thomas Phifer and Partners will consist solely of new gallery space for the museum's collection as part of a larger restructuring of its programs, which include a renovation of its original Edward Durrell Stone building and the 1997 additions by Smith-Miller + Hawkinson and Barbara Kruger. The new building will contain the museum's permanent collection, which includes an important Rodin collection and its European painting collection. The building's morphology is directed toward integrating the building's program, landscape, light, and structure. The mass of the building is penetrated by a variety of garden spaces, which connect interior programs with the Museum of Art's 200-acre park campus. The building is a single story, 26-foot-tall volume with a subterranean level for storage and other support functions. The pavilion organization of the program emphasizes two primary types of integration for the building: maximizing the building's interaction with the surrounding park campus and top lighting for all the galleries.

The pavilion qualities of the building engender both programmatic and material integration with the site. The building's primary circulation route through the historical organization of the museum's collections is punctuated by a set of interspersed gardens. This circulation zone along the edge of the garden spaces thickens the boundary between the galleries and the exterior gardens. In doing so, the zone helps control direct light, glare, ultraviolet radiation, and heat gain. The gardens and reflecting pools were designed with Peter Walker and Partners. The gardens are lined with low-iron glass for maximum transparency between inside and outside. Exterior surfaces that do not face a garden will be clad in stainless steel with an insulated precast concrete substrate. The satin finish of the stainless steel exterior building envelope is highly reflective and is detailed to appear seamless. The cladding will softly reflect the hues of the landscape and sky as visitors move around the building. This most dense of materials, steel, will dematerialize through its dynamic interaction with the light qualities of the site.

Aerial view

OPPOSITE
TOP: Gallery view
BOTTOM: Entry court

The roof surface is also integrated with the performance of the building. In this design, a series of monocoque painted fiberglass vaults are molded with filleted surface transitions, creating even gradient light transitions that avoid the contrast and potential glare of crisp corners. The roof is composed of two layers of fiberglass shells with steel structure, a drainage plane, and other services located in-between. The architects worked closely with Fisher Marantz Stone and daylight engineers in Arup's London office on the daylighting strategy. Each shell coffer contains a single oculus. The oculus will have light-diffusing louvers above it that capture and channel a calibrated amount of light. In the end, only a small percentage of the available light will enter the galleries. These shells give the roof its undulating profile.

The result is a building that works to highly integrate its program and site with directed architectural intentions. Once again, the minimal compositional strategy is paired with maximal performances and effects.

Interior perspectives of galleries and top lighting vaults

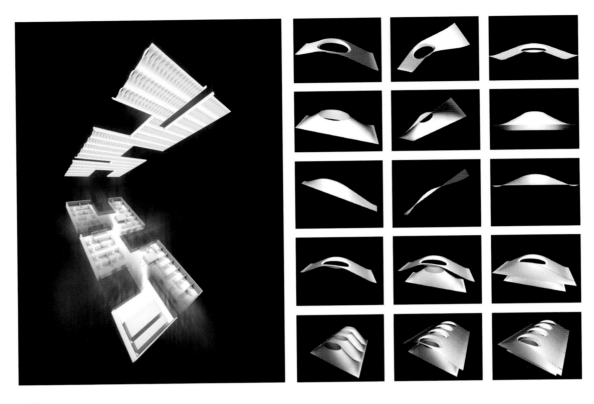

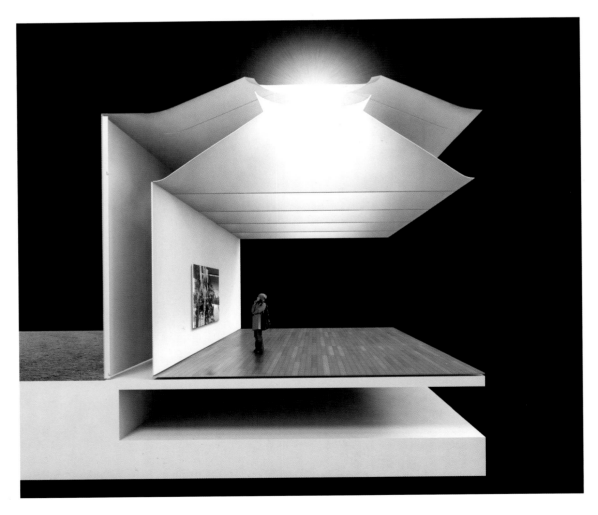

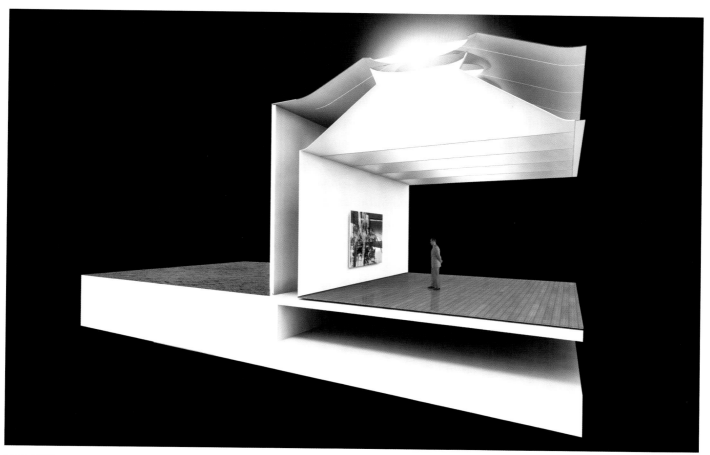

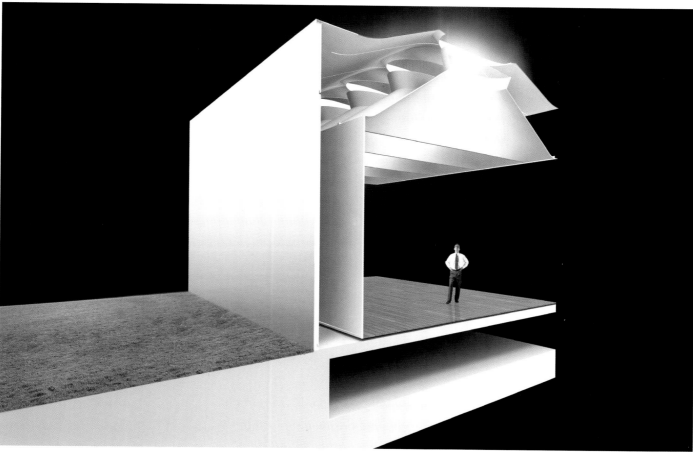

# The Glass Pavilion at the Toledo Museum of Art

Toledo, Ohio

———

Kazuyo Sejima + Ryue Nishizawa: SANAA, Tokyo, Japan

**DESIGN ARCHITECT:** Kazuyo Sejima + Ryue Nishizawa: SANAA: Kazuyo Sejima, Ryue Nishizawa, Principals; Toshihiro Oki, Florian Idenburg, Takayuki Hasegawa, Project Architects; Mizuki Imamura, Junya Ishigami, Hiroshi Kikuchi, Tetsuo Kondo, Keiko Uchiyama, Staff
**ARCHITECT OF RECORD:** Kendall/Heaton Associates: Larry Burns, Nobuhiko Shoga
**DESIGN STRUCTURAL ENGINEER:** SAPS/Sasaki and Partners: Mutsuro Sasaki, Masahiro Ikeda, Eisuke Mitsuda
**STRUCTURAL ENGINEER OF RECORD:** Guy Nordenson and Associates: Guy Nordenson, Brett Schneider
**MECHANICAL, ELECTRICAL, PLUMBING ENGINEER:** Cosentini Associates; Mark Malekshahi, Carmen Ghenta, Anthony Cirillo, Bobby Jaglal
**ENGINEERS/CONSULTANTS:** Project Manager: Paratus Group: Andrew Klemmer, Jon Maass
**CIVIL ENGINEER:** The Mannik & Smith Group
**GEOTECHNICAL ENGINEER:** Bowser-Morner
**LIGHTING CONSULTANT:** Arup: Andrew Sedgwick, Brian Stacy, Andrew McNeil and Kilt Planning Group: Shozo Toyohisa
**COST ESTIMATOR:** Stuart-Lynn Company
**CURTAIN WALL CONSULTANT:** Front: Michael Ra, Marc Simmons, Jeff Kock
**ACOUSTICAL/AV CONSULTANT:** Harvey Marshall Berling Associates: David Harvey
**ELEVATOR CONSULTANT:** Persohn/Hahn Associates
**GENERAL CONTRACTOR:** Rudolph/Libbe
**CFD THERMAL ANALYSIS:** Transsolar: Matthias Schuler
**GRAPHICS DESIGN/SIGNAGE:** 2x4: Michael Rock, Alex Lin, Isreal Kandarian, Manuel Miranda
**CONCRETE CONSULTANT:** Azzarone Contracting: Alan Bouknight
**SECURITY CONSULTANT:** C. H. Guernsey/Layne Consultants & Company
**FOOD SERVICE CONSULTANT:** Gladieux
**LANDSCAPE CONSULTANT:** Neville Tree & Landscape
**GLASSMAKING FACILITY CONSULTANT:** Spiral Arts
**LAMPWORKING CONSULTANT:** Glasscraft
**CASEWORK DESIGNER:** Imrey Culbert
**CURTAIN CONSULTANT:** Inside Outside
**CURTAIN FABRICATOR:** Specialty Drapery

The 76,000-square-foot Glass Pavilion at the Toledo Museum of Art employs integrated design to achieve an emblematic transparency, lightness, and emptiness. The facility contains the museum's glass art collection, temporary exhibition galleries, and an active glass-making production demonstration facility. The pavilion is situated in a park adjacent to the museum and adjacent to a neighborhood of Victorian houses. The extreme transparency of the building continuously connects occupants to the park and the building.

Few surfaces in this building are not performative in some capacity. The 32,000 square feet of raw, low-iron glass in the museum originated in Pilkington's factory in Germany and was sent to Shenzhen, China, for slumping, tempering, laminating, and fabricating into finished panels. The exterior glass uses 122 one-inch-thick laminated units. Thirty of these panels are curved. The interior uses three-quarter-inch laminated unit panels, of which ninety-one are flat and 129 are curved. All of the glass panel connections are dampened, isolating the glass panels from structural deflection and movement.

The architects worked with Guy Nordenson and Associates and SAPS/Sasaki and Partners on the conception and execution of the structure. The minimal structure also demands unique solutions. Three and a half-inch to four and a quarter-inch diameter steel columns carry vertical loads to the concrete plinth-and-mat foundation. Most of these columns are solid steel. Exposed three-quarter-inch steel plates in the lampworking room and diagonal bracing embedded in opaque walls constitute the building's lateral load system.

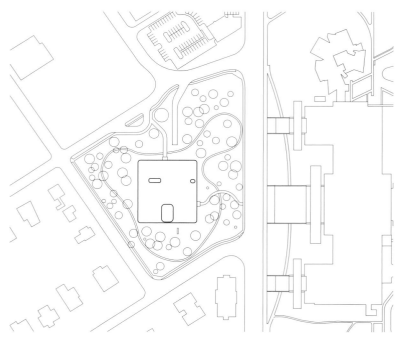

Site plan

OPPOSITE
Plans and elevations

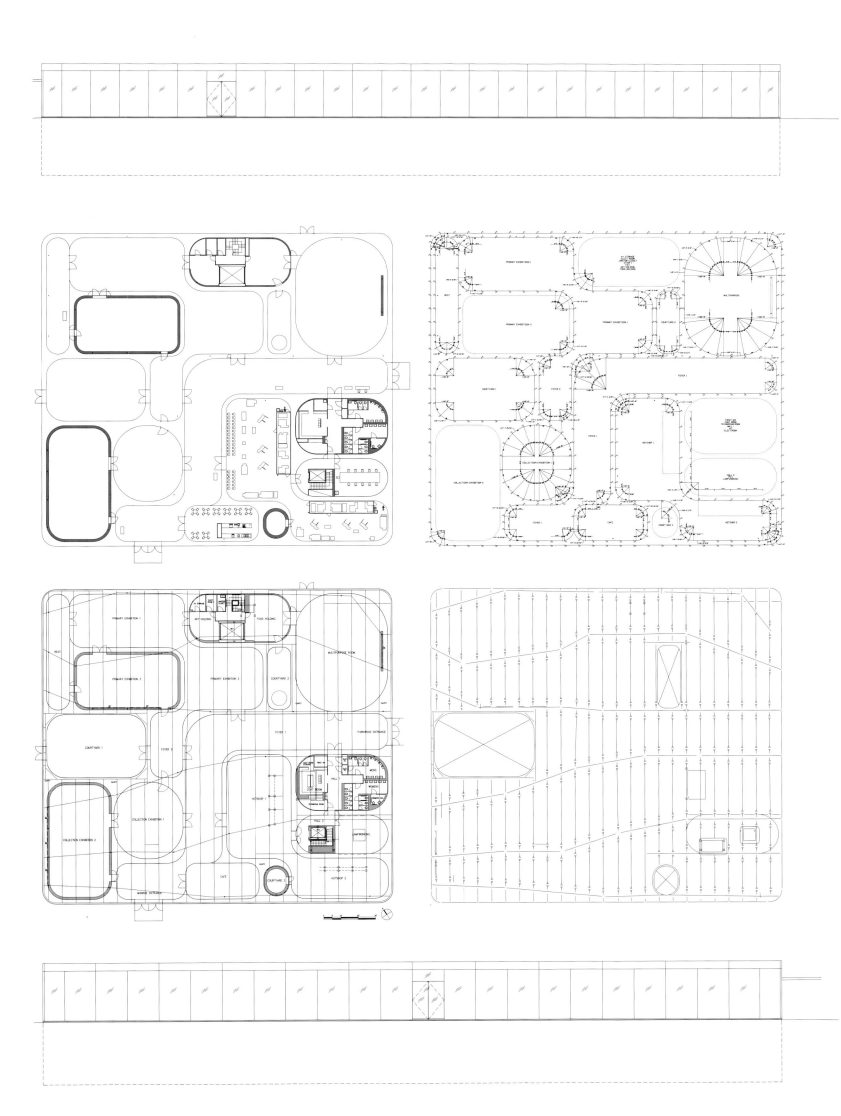

Transsolar was central to the conception of the building's energy strategies. The building has three primary energy zones. The first is the interstitial thermal buffer between the exterior glass envelope and interior zones. This zone is tempered by hydronic radiant heating and cooling in the floor and ceiling of the buffer space. The radiant energy tempers the surface temperature of the inside and outside glass and therefore minimizes the buffer space air supply and temperature. This prevents the formation of condensation on the glass surfaces throughout the year. The second zone is the hot zone of the glass production facility. Heat from this space is recovered through a hydronic floor slab and used elsewhere in the facility, including the hydronic exterior loading ramp slab that cuts down through the site to the basement. The third zone consists of the discrete gallery zones that have more specific air temperature and humidity requirements for the permanent and temporary exhibitions. The cool air from the galleries is recovered and used to cool the hot glass production zone.

Curtains are increasingly intense technical devices in many contemporary integrated design solutions. In the buffer spaces on specific orientations, the curtains reflect incident solar radiation with aluminum flakes (Verosol) on the exterior surfaces of the curtain thereby minimizing direct solar gain while engendering a diaphanous, muted light in the interiors. Reduced densities at the top and bottom of the curtains ventilate the solar gain captured between the outside surface of the curtain and the exterior glass. Extensive light studies throughout the year determined the placement and extent of the curtains for various program spaces.

The roof assembly is one tightly integrated zone of the building. A CATIA digital model was generated to test for interferences amongst the roof structure, fire systems, lighting systems, and roof drains. Structurally, the primary girders could not be punctured, so all services run through holes in the middle of the secondary beams. After the structure was installed, the structure was surveyed to test for low spots. Certain portions of the structure were jacked up while high spots were adjusted to accommodate the appropriate roof slope.

The building is a prime example of the maximal within the minimal that is characteristic of integrated design. There is a tendency for every component, every surface to perform multiple functions.

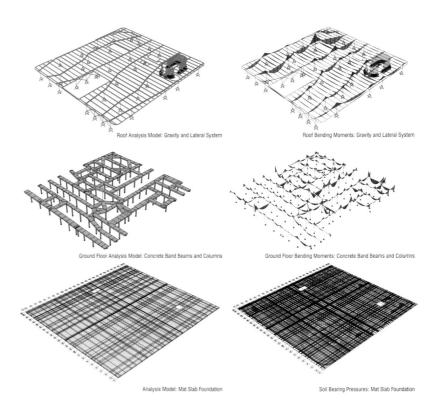

Roof Analysis Model: Gravity and Lateral System

Roof Bending Moments: Gravity and Lateral System

Ground Floor Analysis Model: Concrete Band Beams and Columns

Ground Floor Bending Moments: Concrete Band Beams and Columns

Analysis Model: Mat Slab Foundation

Soil Bearing Pressures: Mat Slab Foundation

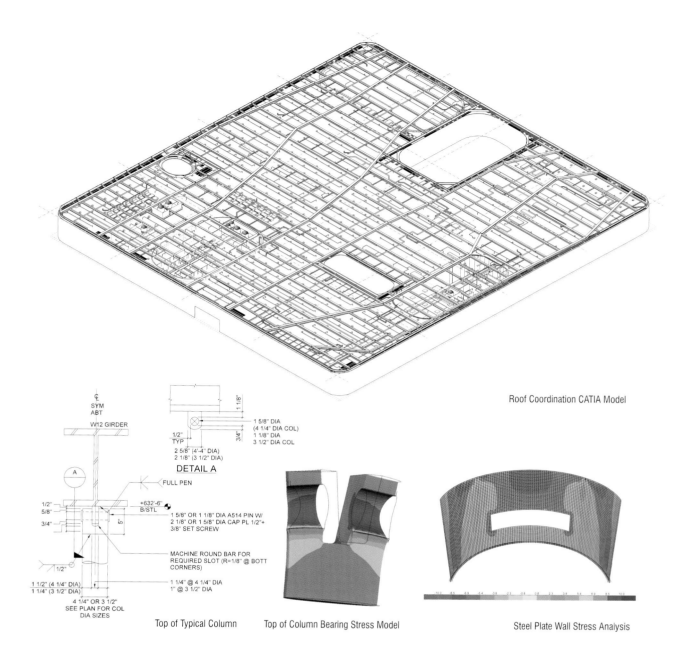

Roof Coordination CATIA Model

## DETAIL A

SYM
ABT

W12 GIRDER

1 1/8"

1 5/8" DIA
(4 1/4" DIA COL)
1 1/8" DIA
3 1/2" DIA COL

1/2"
TYP

3/4"

2 5/8" (4'-4" DIA)
2 1/8" (3 1/2" DIA)

Ⓐ

FULL PEN

1/2"
5/8"
3/4"

+632'-6"
B/STL

1 5/8" OR 1 1/8" DIA A514 PIN W/
2 1/8" OR 1 5/8" DIA CAP PL 1/2"+
3/8" SET SCREW

5"

MACHINE ROUND BAR FOR
REQUIRED SLOT (R=1/8" @ BOTT
CORNERS)

1/2"

1 1/2" (4 1/4" DIA)
1 1/4" (3 1/2" DIA)

1 1/4" @ 4 1/4" DIA
1" @ 3 1/2" DIA

4 1/4" OR 3 1/2"
SEE PLAN FOR COL
DIA SIZES

Top of Typical Column

Top of Column Bearing Stress Model

Steel Plate Wall Stress Analysis

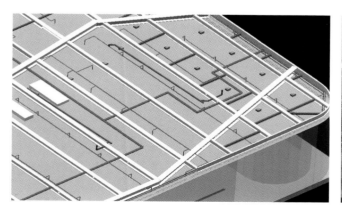

107

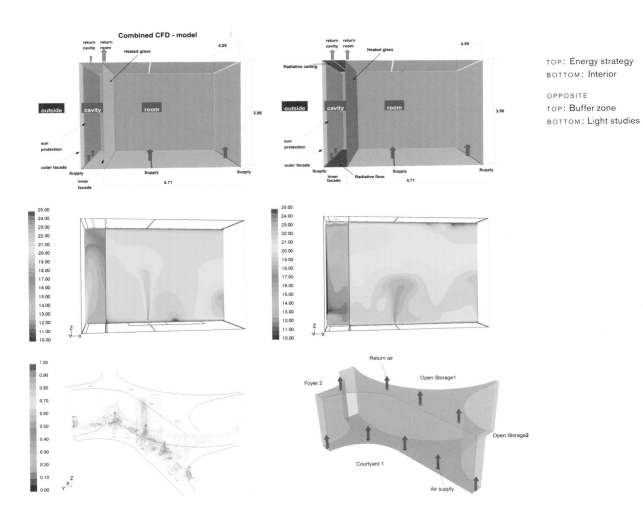

**Combined CFD - model**

TOP : Energy strategy
BOTTOM : Interior

OPPOSITE
TOP : Buffer zone
BOTTOM : Light studies

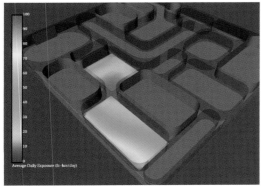

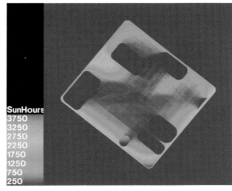

TOP: Glass details
BOTTOM: Glass radii and base section

OPPOSITE
TOP: Glass details
BOTTOM: Envelope detail

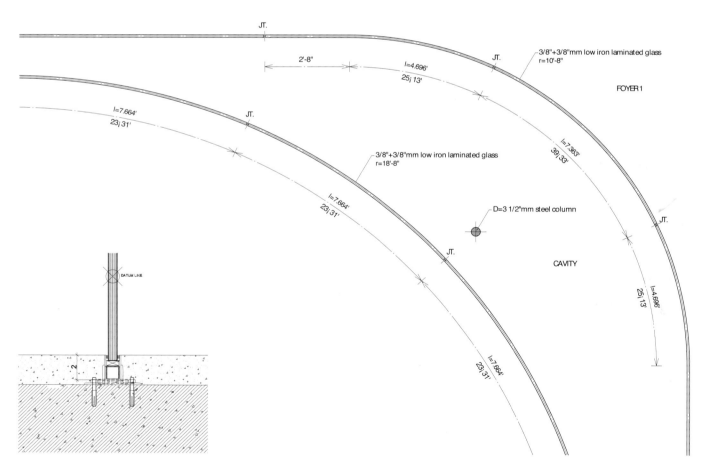

JT.

2'-8"

l=4.696'
25¡13'

JT.

3/8"+3/8"mm low iron laminated glass
r=10'-8"

FOYER 1

l=7.664'
23¡31'

JT.

l=7.363'
39¡33'

3/8"+3/8"mm low iron laminated glass
r=18'-8"

l=7.664'
23¡31'

D=3 1/2"mm steel column

JT.

JT.

l=4.696'
25¡13'

CAVITY

l=7.664'
23¡31'

DATUM LINE

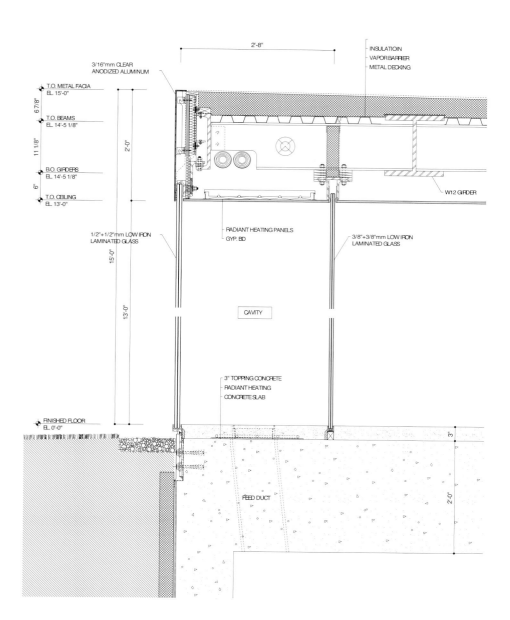

INSULATIOIN
VAPOR BARRIER
METAL DECKING

3/16"mm CLEAR
ANODIZED ALUMINUM

T.O. METAL FACIA
EL. 15'-0"

6 7/8"

T.O. BEAMS
EL. 14'-5 1/8"

11 1/8"

B.O. GIRDERS
EL. 14'-5 1/8"

6"

T.O. CEILING
EL. 13'-0"

2'-8"

2'-0"

W12 GIRDER

1/2"+1/2"mm LOW IRON
LAMINATED GLASS

RADIANT HEATING PANELS
GYP. BD

3/8"+3/8"mm LOW IRON
LAMINATED GLASS

15'-0"

13'-0"

CAVITY

3" TOPPING CONCRETE
RADIANT HEATING
CONCRETE SLAB

FINISHED FLOOR
EL. 0'-0"

3"

FEED DUCT

2'-0"

# Crown Hall Renovation, Illinois Institute of Technology

Chicago, Illinois

———

Krueck & Sexton Architects, Chicago, Illinois

ARCHITECT: Krueck & Sexton Architects
ASSOCIATE ARCHITECTS AND FIRMS: McClier Preservation Group (now Austin AECOM): Fred Borisch; Fujikawa Johnson Gobel Architects: Gregory Gobel
STRUCTURAL SOUTH PORCH: Thorton Tomasetti
MECHANICAL, ELECRTICAL, PLUMBING AND STRUCTURAL ENGINEER: Austin AECOM
ENVIRONMENTAL: Atelier Ten and Transsolar Energietechnik GmbH
GENERAL CONTRACTOR: Clune Construction Company
OWNER: Illinois Institute of Technology
OWNER, SITE VISIT CONTACT: Donna Robertson, FAIA
PHOTOGRAPHER: Todd Eberle Photography and Ron Gordon Photo

After fifty years of use, Mies van der Rohe's S. R. Crown Hall at the Illinois Institute of Technology underwent a renovation, both for necessary maintenance as well as to update the facility for contemporary needs: increased enrollment, new technologies, Americans with Disabilities Act (ADA) compliance, and repro-gramming. The renovation alters some assumptions about the perceived relationships between site, energy, and building performance of a high modernist, such as Mies.

The renovation work began with analysis by an architecture, preservation, glazing, sustainability, engineering, and construction team. Atelier Ten and Transsolar Energietechnik conducted a climatic and systems analysis of the building's original design, which highlighted several passive techniques of the original composition: daylighting, solar-control trees around the building, and radiant heating. Intervening attempts at renovation in the seventies compromised these original strategies. Changed and increased uses in the building, along with some detrimental modifications only exasperated the problems of the building's current performance. The building experienced overheating in the summer, chill in the winter, glare, ventilation issues, and asymmetrical heating loads.

The approach for the renovation was to restore a number of the original strategies and amend others with new techniques and technologies. Zoning is a simple, but important, strategy for the glass enclosed box. In the renovation, various zones can respond to the differential heat loads evident in the space between the southwest and northeast corners, for example. The original building envelope was limited in its ability to modulate the internal milieu. Internal blinds and low operable vents along the bottom of the glazed wall permitted minor, albeit unreliable,

modulations. Much of the renovation work focused on the building envelope. The steel was sandblasted to bare metal and finished with epoxy paint. A significant upgrade to the building included the replacement of the glazing from an earlier renovation with laminated glazing units that are sandblasted, like the original glass, but also have an interior laminate that modulates the energy absorbance and transmittance of the glass. The upper panes are thicker, low-iron glass, thereby improving its energy and visual performance. An analysis on the original glass, replacement glass from a renovation in the seventies, and the new glazing represents a significant performance improvement.

The stature of this seminal building restricted the type of interventions. The detailing of the new, thicker glazing prompted much attention and was developed through a rigorous design review committee that included former Mies employees on the faculty. The glazing stops maintain the original 5/8-inch-thick frame appearance from the outside but use a slightly pitched top block that helps shed water, greatly improving the detail performance and durability. Other new performance strategies aim to preserve the visual appearance of the original building. One forthcoming and discrete strategy is low-emission paint for the ceiling of the building's large upper volume, which will retain more heat in the winter than the existing ceiling surface. Another strategy will use the original hydronic strategy for heating and cooling with four discrete zones to provide more control with less energy consumption. All together, the renovation cuts the building's energy use in half while greatly improving human comfort and maintaining or restoring Mies's original details and systems.

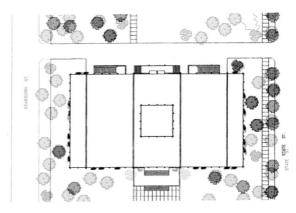

Site plan with original and current trees

OPPOSITE
TOP: Renovation enclosure
BOTTOM: Renovated south entrance

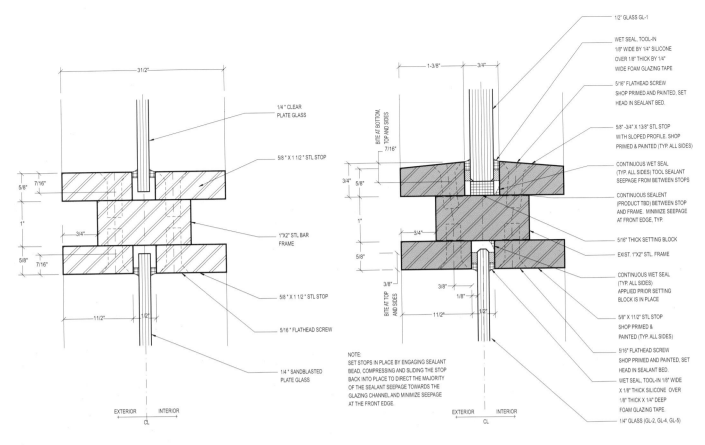

**Detail 1 labels (left, Original Design):**

- 31/2"
- 1/4" CLEAR PLATE GLASS
- 5/8" X 1 1/2" STL STOP
- 5/8", 7/16"
- 1"X2" STL BAR FRAME
- 1"
- 3/4"
- 5/8", 7/16"
- 11/2", 1/2"
- 5/8" X 1 1/2" STL STOP
- 5/16" FLATHEAD SCREW
- 1/4" SANDBLASTED PLATE GLASS
- EXTERIOR / INTERIOR — CL

**Detail 2 labels (right, Restoration Design):**

- 1-3/8", 3/4"
- 1/2" GLASS GL-1
- WET SEAL, TOOL-IN 1/8" WIDE BY 1/4" SILICONE OVER 1/8" THICK BY 1/4" WIDE FOAM GLAZING TAPE
- BITE AT BOTTOM, TOP AND SIDES
- 7/16"
- 5/16" FLATHEAD SCREW SHOP PRIMED AND PAINTED, SET HEAD IN SEALANT BED.
- 5/8" -3/4" X 13/8" STL STOP WITH SLOPED PROFILE. SHOP PRIMED & PAINTED (TYP. ALL SIDES)
- 3/4", 5/8"
- CONTINUOUS WET SEAL (TYP. ALL SIDES) TOOL SEALANT SEEPAGE FROM BETWEEN STOPS
- 1"
- CONTINUOUS SEALENT (PRODUCT TBD) BETWEEN STOP AND FRAME. MINIMIZE SEEPAGE AT FRONT EDGE, TYP.
- 3/4"
- 5/16" THICK SETTING BLOCK
- 5/8"
- EXIST. 1"X2" STL. FRAME
- BITE AT TOP AND SIDES
- 3/8", 3/8"
- CONTINUOUS WET SEAL (TYP. ALL SIDES) APPLIED PRIOR SETTING BLOCK IS IN PLACE
- 1/8"
- 5/8" X 11/2" STL STOP SHOP PRIMED & PAINTED (TYP. ALL SIDES)
- 11/2", 1/2"
- 5/16" FLATHEAD SCREW SHOP PRIMED AND PAINTED, SET HEAD IN SEALANT BED.
- WET SEAL, TOOL-IN 1/8" WIDE X 1/8" THICK SILICONE OVER 1/8" THICK X 1/4" DEEP FOAM GLAZING TAPE.
- 1/4" GLASS (GL-2, GL-4, GL-5)
- EXTERIOR / INTERIOR — CL

NOTE:
SET STOPS IN PLACE BY ENGAGING SEALANT BEAD, COMPRESSING AND SLIDING THE STOP BACK INTO PLACE TO DIRECT THE MAJORITY OF THE SEALANT SEEPAGE TOWARDS THE GLAZING CHANNEL AND MINIMIZE SEEPAGE AT THE FRONT EDGE.

1. SR Crown Hall Window Wall Detail
Original Design

2. SR Crown Hall Window Wall Detail
Restoration Design

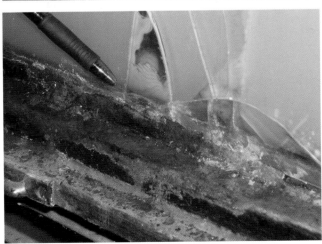

Building envelope renovation

OPPOSITE
TOP: Original and renovated
glazing stop detail
BOTTOM: Condition of
building envelope before
restoration

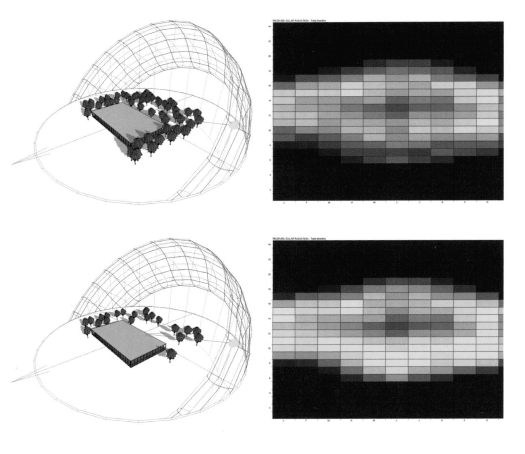

TOP: Crown Hall landscape solar control
BOTTOM: Summer and winter performance for original building and subsequent renovations

OPPOSITE
TOP: Original, 1970s renovated, and new glass performance
MIDDLE: Low-emission paint and new radiant floor zones
BOTTOM: Enlarged Climate Concept for Summer

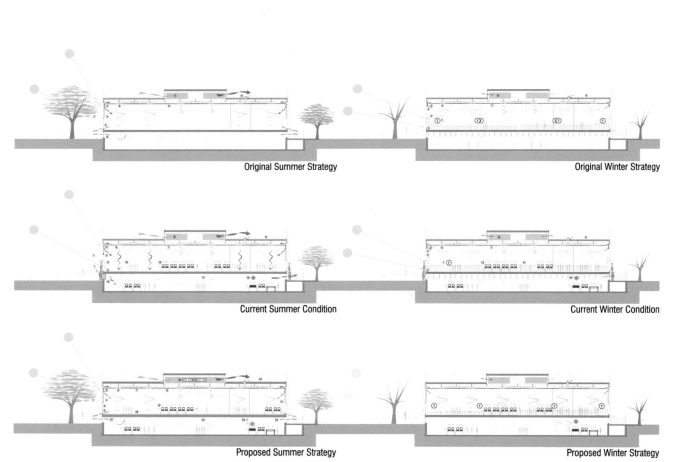

Original Summer Strategy

Original Winter Strategy

Current Summer Condition

Current Winter Condition

Proposed Summer Strategy

Proposed Winter Strategy

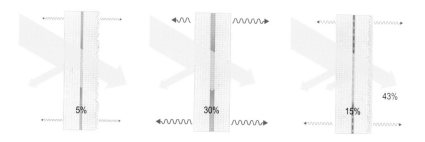

5%          30%          15%          43%

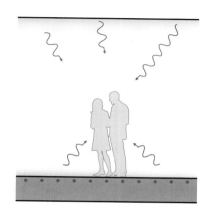
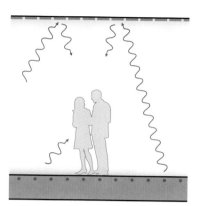

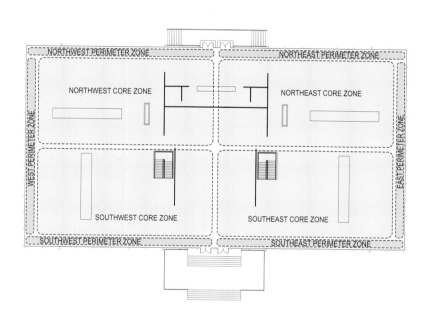

NORTHWEST PERIMETER ZONE                    NORTHEAST PERIMETER ZONE

NORTHWEST CORE ZONE          NORTHEAST CORE ZONE

SOUTHWEST CORE ZONE          SOUTHEAST CORE ZONE

WEST PERIMETER ZONE          EAST PERIMETER ZONE

SOUTHWEST PERIMETER ZONE                    SOUTHEAST PERIMETER ZONE

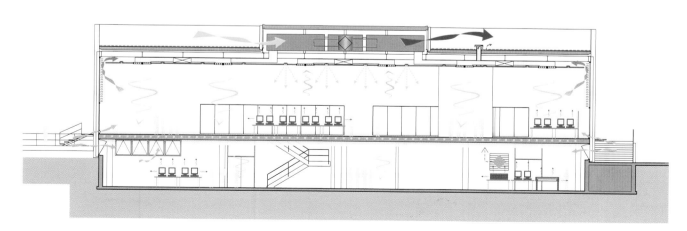

# Lavin-Bernick Center for University Life

Tulane University, New Orleans, Louisiana

VJAA with James Carpenter Design Associates and Transsolar Energietechnik

ARCHITECT: VJAA in association with James Carpenter
Design Associates and Transsolar Energietechnick
GmbH: Project Team: Vincent James, Jennifer Yoos,
Nathan Knutson, Managing Principal; Paul Yaggie, Project
Architect; Carl Gauley, Lev Bereznycky, Karen Lu, Steven
Philippi, Andrew Dull, Taavo Somer, Bob Loken, James
Moore, Dzenita Hadziomerovic, Donovan Nelson, Mark
Searls, Malini Srivastava, Dan Clark, Casey Renner, Aaron
Roseth, Eric Whittington, Matthew Hutchinson
CONSULTING ARCHITECT: Wayne Troyer Architect, Louisiana
STRUCTURAL AND CIVIL ENGINEERING: Kulkarni Consultants,
Louisiana
MECHANICAL, ELECTRICAL, AND PLUMBING: Moses
Engineers, Louisiana
LANDSCAPE ARCHITECT: Coen + Partners
DAYLIGHTING AND GLAZING CONSULTANT: James Carpenter
Design Associates
JCDA TEAM: James Carpenter, Richard Kress, Rayme
Kuniyuki, Dietmar Geiselmann, Joe Welker, Ulrike Franzel,
Henrike Bosbach, Marek Walczak
CLIMATE ENGINEERING: Matthias Schuler; Transsolar
Energietchnik GmbH, Stuttgart
CONSULTING ENGINEER (PREDESIGN PHASE): Arup,
New York
CONSTRUCTION ADMINISTRATION: Chris Goad (WTA),
Lev Bereznycky (VJAA)
PHOTOGRAPHER: Paul Crosby

At Tulane University's renovated 150,000-square-foot Lavin-Bernick Center for University Life, VJAA reprogrammed both the social and environmental functions of an existing student center. The architects merged social programming with particular climate concepts to yield a porous climatic and social milieu that reverses the hermetically sealed strategy of the original building.

VJAA used architectural strategies familiar to the New Orleans area, such as exterior porches, canopies, balconies, louvered shading devices, and architectural-scale fans to temper the porous space. These strategies reduce energy consumption while prompting exchanges of people, light, and air between the interior and exterior. In this case, the building envelope is not what distinguishes inside and outside, but rather is best understood as a zone in which change occurs. The envelope is conceptually not a line but a gradient of social and climatic intensities. The building envelope is defined more by its behavior, rather than the objects and components that constitute it.

Zoning is an important concept in this project. The architects strategically align, overlap, and separate programmatic and environmental zones to enable the various climatic strategies. Private zones with discrete environmental control parameters are separated from the more open public spaces that merge with the exterior and thus have more variable environmental conditions.

The architects worked with Transsolar Energietechnik to develop the building's climate and energy concepts. A building management system regulates psychrometric conditions, supplying ventilation and air conditioning as required. An elaborate sun-shading device wraps the building's sun exposures, modulating interior light levels throughout while lowering incident heat gain. The density of the shading system is correlated to the program of space beyond the shade. Vegetated walls also help shade portions of the building. Three sixty-foot-long clerestory stacks over the central space drop light into the core of the building while the sun heats up its upper surfaces, exaggerating the buoyant air flow in this space. Pendulum paddle fans typical of New Orleans vernacular buildings are deployed in the commons to push air toward two water walls. Water walls passively dehumidify the New Orleans air while hydronic radiant cooling ceilings lower the operative temperature of the space and thus the demand for power-operated air conditioning. The water for the water walls is from the central plant and its temperature is lower than the ambient air dew point as another radiant, heat absorbing surface.

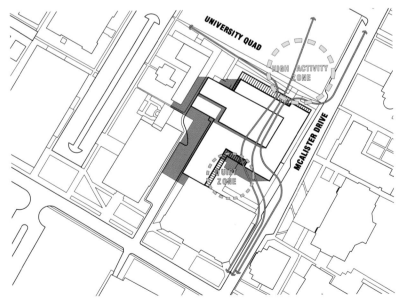

Site plan

OPPOSITE
TOP: Exterior during the day
BOTTOM: Exterior at night

In other areas, low-energy ceiling fans recirculate cool supply air back down to the occupied zone and induce turbulence in the air flow. A perforated metal ceiling throughout the spaces functions as a diffuser for dehumidified air as well as a light and acoustic modulator. The architects' representational studies focus on the behavior of light and its interaction with the ceiling plane by using gradients of light energy, once again calibrating energy performance with respective zones beyond. Following Hurricane Katrina, Tulane University now sees this project as a model for building strategies for the campus and region.

TOP: Section at daylight and ventilation stack
BOTTOM: Student center from campus quad

OPPOSITE
Plans and section

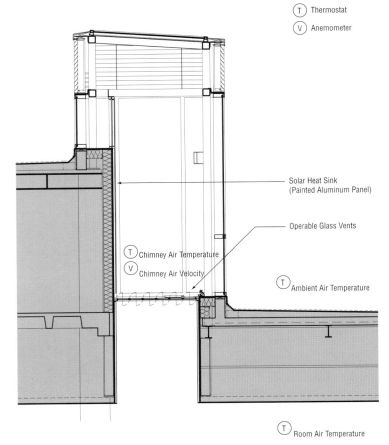

Thermostat
Anemometer
Solar Heat Sink (Painted Aluminum Panel)
Operable Glass Vents
Chimney Air Temperature
Chimney Air Velocity
Ambient Air Temperature
Room Air Temperature

If building doors are open, and Room Air temperature is greater than Ambient Internal Air Temperature, then operable glass vents will open allowing the solar chimney to exhaust hot air.

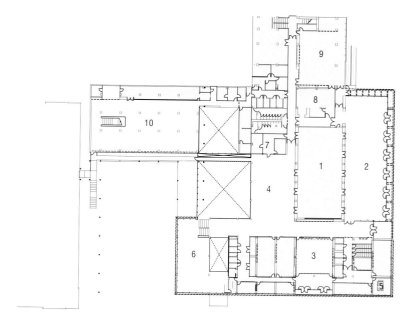

Second-level plan

Second-level plan

1 Glass ballroom / Lecture hall
2 Ballroom terrace
3 Meeting / Conference rooms
4 Prefunction space / Study lounge
5 Conference rooms
6 Mezzanine
7 Building services
8 Catering
9 Faculty staff dining lobby
10 Bookstore

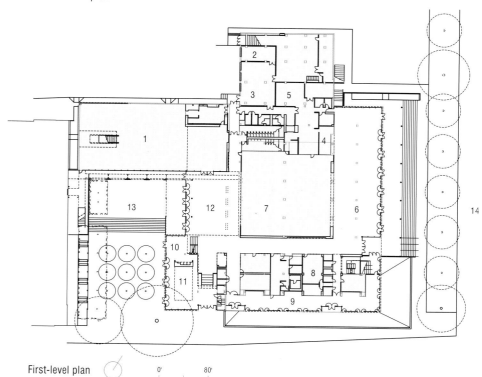

First-level plan

1 Bookstore
2 Mechanical and electrical room
3 Kitchen
4 Dishroom
5 Food preparation area
6 Main dining hall
7 Food service
8 Commercial service
9 Study / Computer lounge
10 Lounge
11 Coffee bar / Deli
12 Commons
13 Courtyard
14 Campus Quad

First-level plan

0'          80'

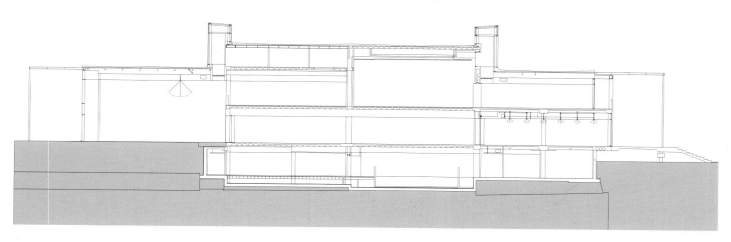

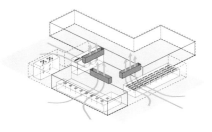

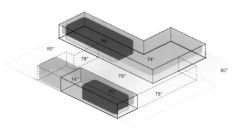

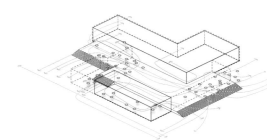

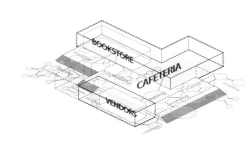

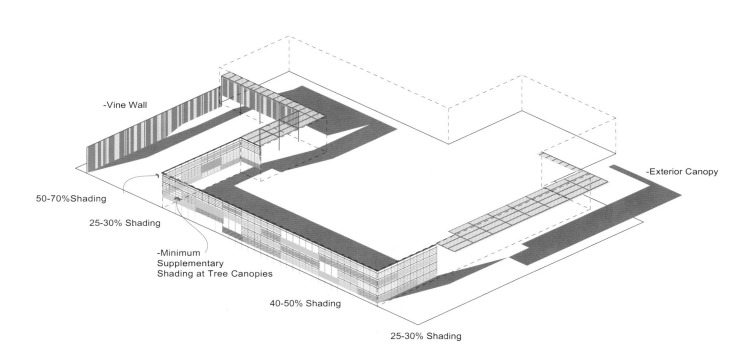

-Vine Wall

-Exterior Canopy

50-70% Shading

25-30% Shading

-Minimum Supplementary Shading at Tree Canopies

40-50% Shading

25-30% Shading

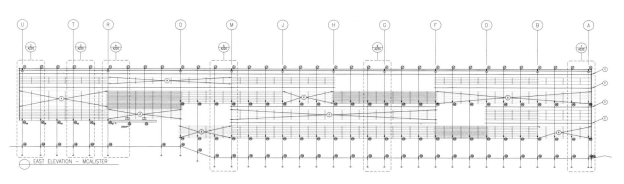

EAST ELEVATION - MCALISTER

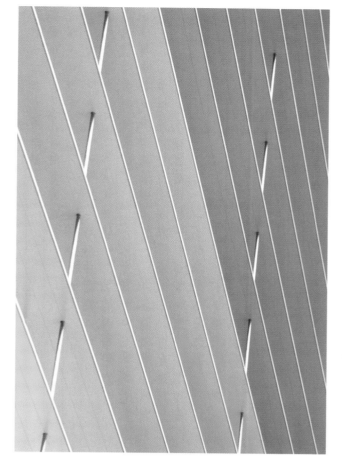

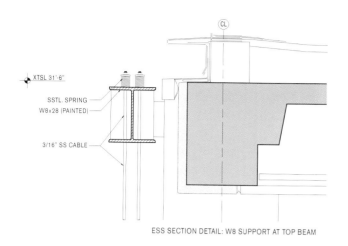

XTSL 31'-6"

SSTL. SPRING
W8x28 (PAINTED)

3/16" SS CABLE

ESS SECTION DETAIL: W8 SUPPORT AT TOP BEAM

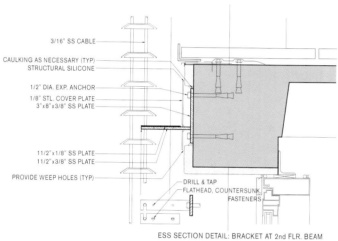

3/16" SS CABLE

CAULKING AS NECESSARY (TYP)
STRUCTURAL SILICONE

1/2" DIA. EXP. ANCHOR
1/8" STL. COVER PLATE
3"x8"x3/8" SS PLATE

11/2"x1/8" SS PLATE
11/2"x3/8" SS PLATE

PROVIDE WEEP HOLES (TYP)

DRILL & TAP
FLATHEAD, COUNTERSUNK
FASTENERS

ESS SECTION DETAIL: BRACKET AT 2nd FLR. BEAM

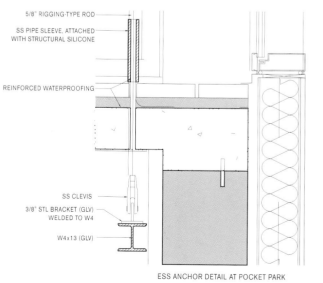

5/8" RIGGING-TYPE ROD

SS PIPE SLEEVE, ATTACHED
WITH STRUCTURAL SILICONE

REINFORCED WATERPROOFING

SS CLEVIS
3/8" STL BRACKET (GLV)
WELDED TO W4

W4x13 (GLV)

ESS ANCHOR DETAIL AT POCKET PARK

TOP: Reflected ceiling plan
BOTTOM: Interior view

OPPOSITE
TOP: Interior view of
perforated metal panels
BOTTOM: Interior view with
paddle fans

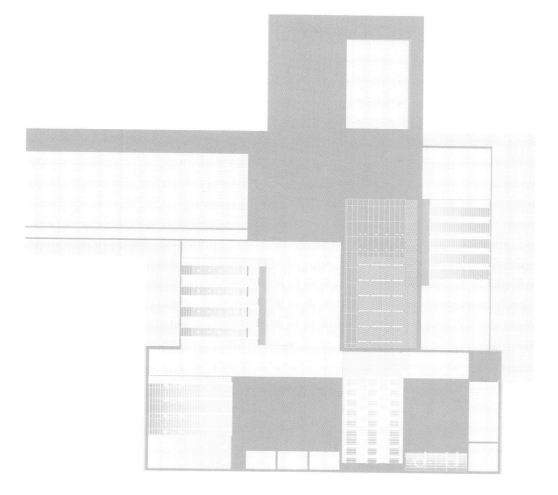

TOP: Water wall
MIDDLE: Fan assembly
detailed
BELOW: Details of water wall

OPPOSITE
Water wall view

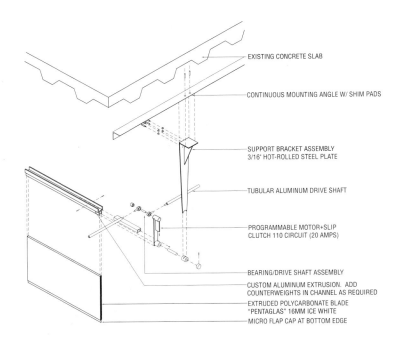

EXISTING CONCRETE SLAB

CONTINUOUS MOUNTING ANGLE W/ SHIM PADS

SUPPORT BRACKET ASSEMBLY
3/16" HOT-ROLLED STEEL PLATE

TUBULAR ALUMINUM DRIVE SHAFT

PROGRAMMABLE MOTOR+SLIP
CLUTCH 110 CIRCUIT (20 AMPS)

BEARING/DRIVE SHAFT ASSEMBLY

CUSTOM ALUMINUM EXTRUSION. ADD
COUNTERWEIGHTS IN CHANNEL AS REQUIRED

EXTRUDED POLYCARBONATE BLADE
"PENTAGLAS" 16MM ICE WHITE

MICRO FLAP CAP AT BOTTOM EDGE

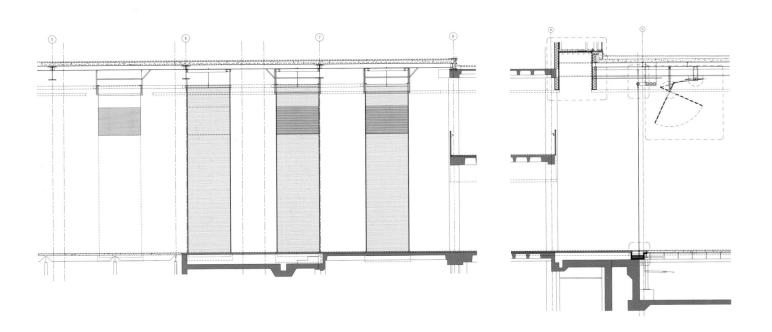

# Seminar II Building at the Evergreen State College

Olympia, Washington

---

Mahlum Architects, Seattle, Washington

ARCHITECT: Anne Schopf, Design Partner;
Mark Cork AIA, Project architect
STRUCTURAL ENGINEER: Martens/Chan (now AHBL)
MECHANICAL ENGINEER: Keen Engineering (now Stantec)
LANDSCAPE ARCHITECT: Murase Associates
CIVIL ENGINEER: SvR Design Company
LIGHTING DESIGNER: Candela
ENVIRONMENTAL BUILDING CONSULTANT: Paladino &
Company; Wood Harbinger
ELECTRICAL ENGINEER: Sparling

The Evergreen State College Seminar II Building emerged from a highly participatory design process that reflects the highly interdisciplinary instruction and environmental orientation of the college. The participatory nature of the project extended to the bidding phase as well with a conference to inform potential contractors of their role in the project's integrated ambitions. Thus the social construction of this project is directly related to the physical construction of the project.

The 165,000-square-foot program breaks up into five clustered buildings on the edge of the campus, which are interdigitated with the adjacent forest. This provides a small scale to the buildings and abundant views into the forest for each building. Each building contains seminar rooms, a lecture hall, faculty offices, a workshop, and student homerooms. Faculty and students spend extended periods of time together in the building. This, along with the environmental orientation of the college, demanded high human comfort with minimal energy strategies.

Each building has two primary zones when viewed in section. The ground level lecture hall and meeting rooms are mechanically ventilated. The upper three floors utilize perimeter hydronic radiators and an air-and-light stack to modulate human comfort. This sectional arrangement enables fresh-air strategies for the building while avoiding problematic code issues. The interdigitated plan composition maximizes not only views, but fresh air as well. Thus nearly all glazing in the buildings is operable. Together, these strategies allow 80 percent of the building to be ventilated without mechanical systems. The building also uses light shelves in faculty offices and aluminum louvers on southern exposures to control and direct day light. All occupied spaces in the building have natural day light. The porosity of the section amplifies human interaction and interior visual connections amongst the program clusters.

The concrete structure provides excellent thermal mass and highly durable (100 year) construction. A night time purge ventilation strategy utilizes the exposed thermal mass to cool the building in the summer. The exposed concrete also forms durable finish surfaces throughout the building, obviating the need for additional layers of construction. Other material specifications included locally available and harvested materials such as alder and reclaimed maple. Material systems typically remain elemental and tend to avoid superfluous layers.

Water is an activating agent for this Pacific Northwest project. Vegetated roofs cover half of the roof area. A stormwater control system is integrated in the building and adjacent landscape to yield no net increase in stormwater runoff into the adjacent Thornton Creek Watershed. Stormwater is channeled from the roofs through runnels in the landscaped courtyards in between the clustered buildings. The landscape strategy focuses on native species that are sun, shade, and drought tolerant and thus require no additional irrigation.

Taken together, the strategies employed here evidence the view that buildings are determined more by their dynamic interaction with their surrounding milieu and contexts than a building's own objecthood. Here the building is an active device for capturing and channeling views, the adjacent landscape, air, energy, and water.

Clustered site strategy with
interdigitated forest edge

OPPOSITE
Exterior view

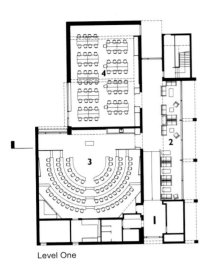

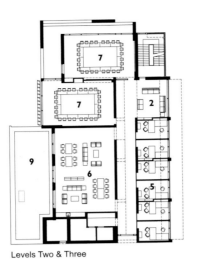

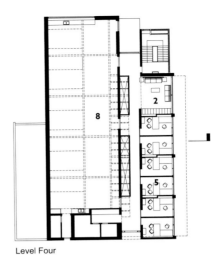

Level One

Levels Two & Three

Level Four

1 Entry
2 Break-out
3 Lecture Hall

4 Workshop
5 Offices
6 Homeroom

7 Seminar Room
8 Class Lab
9 Vegetated Roof

0    8'   16'      32'

TOP: Plans
BOTTOM: Light and views
in a break-out room

OPPOSITE
TOP: Building section
BOTTOM LEFT: Light, air,
and view Stack
BOTTOM RIGHT: Seminar
room

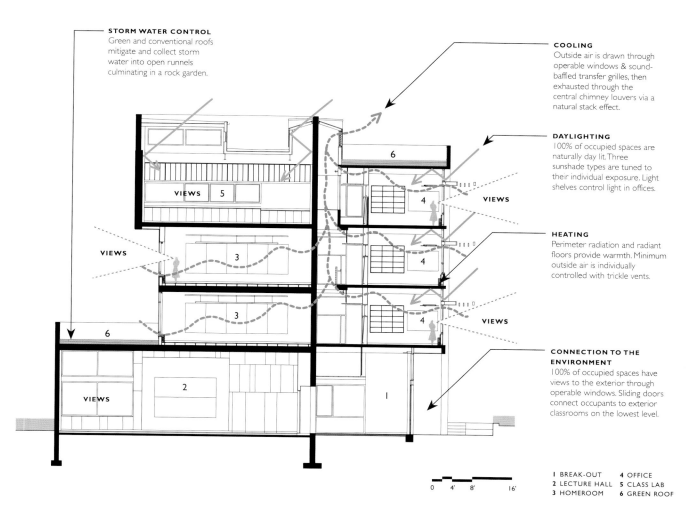

**STORM WATER CONTROL**
Green and conventional roofs mitigate and collect storm water into open runnels culminating in a rock garden.

**COOLING**
Outside air is drawn through operable windows & sound-baffled transfer grilles, then exhausted through the central chimney louvers via a natural stack effect.

**DAYLIGHTING**
100% of occupied spaces are naturally day lit. Three sunshade types are tuned to their individual exposure. Light shelves control light in offices.

**HEATING**
Perimeter radiation and radiant floors provide warmth. Minimum outside air is individually controlled with trickle vents.

**CONNECTION TO THE ENVIRONMENT**
100% of occupied spaces have views to the exterior through operable windows. Sliding doors connect occupants to exterior classrooms on the lowest level.

0    4'    8'        16'

| | |
|---|---|
| **1** BREAK-OUT | **4** OFFICE |
| **2** LECTURE HALL | **5** CLASS LAB |
| **3** HOMEROOM | **6** GREEN ROOF |

TOP: Vegetated roof and skylight vent
BOTTOM: Exterior view

OPPOSITE
TOP LEFT: Roof overflow and surface runnel
TOP RIGHT: Solar-control
BOTTOM LEFT: Building and landscape
BOTTOM RIGHT: Building, flora, and fauna

# Milton Academy Science Building

Milton, Massachusetts

The Rose + Guggenheimer Studio, Cambridge, Massachusetts, and New York, New York

**ARCHITECT:** The Rose + Guggenheimer Studio
**STRUCTURAL ENGINEER:** Richmond So Engineers
**MECHANICAL, ELECTRICAL, PLUMBING ENGINEER:**
Ambrosino, DePinto and Schmeider
**LIGHTING CONSULTANT:** Tillotson Design Associates
**OWNER:** Milton Academy
**ENVIRONMENTAL ENGINEER:** Transsolar Energietechnik
GmbH
**LAB PLANNERS:** GPR Planners Collaborative, now Jacobs
Consultancy

The Milton Academy Science Building amplifies the inquiry-based pedagogy of Milton Academy. One aim was to put science on display through both the building's transparency and through its building science performance, which directly informs the building's composition. The building is deftly situated on the Milton campus in such a way that it creates three separate courtyards and funnels a variety of circulation routes throughout the campus into its central atrium. This prompts students to engage with each other and with science. An atrium separates parallel bars of laboratory programs. The lowest level on the north side contains an auditorium, fabrication shop, and support spaces. The north and south bars are slightly offset when seen in section. This configuration emphasizes cross-section views and engenders more dynamic circulation routes through the atrium. The bottom side of the concrete stairs and bridges in the atrium are figured by a pattern related to the structural forces for each of the various spans.

The atrium is a critical aspect of the scheme's organization and operation. It provides a unifying circulation space for light, air, and people. The atrium directs light into the depth of the building, aided by automated louvers that control the luminous energy. The atrium also channels exhaust air through buoyancy out through the top skylight assembly. Fresh air is drawn in low on the exterior envelope and high on the atrium side of the program bars. For a laboratory building, this ventilation strategy is augmented by a zone of ducts that runs cleanly above each laboratory and distributes air, water, and fire sprinklers. The east and west ends of the atrium contain low operable glazing that fully vents the atrium space, reducing the required mechanical plant. The building utilizes thermally active slabs for hydronic heating and cooling. This minimizes the mechanical plant and infrastructure. The architects worked with Transsolar Energietechnik to develop and test these performative aspects of the building.

The building envelope section demonstrates the clear separation of the thermal envelope and the cast-in-place concrete building structure, a critical principle for building envelope durability and energy efficiency while yielding the desired taut, transparent envelope. The exterior envelope consists of an operable curtain wall with exterior, automated profile shades that continually adjust to the sun's position in order to provide a consistent and comfortable level of illumination in the lab spaces. There is focus on durable, serviceable, and adaptable systems throughout the building. The laboratories are configured as loft spaces with modular furniture and service systems that facilitate programmatic adaptability over time while exposed mechanical systems foster serviceability. The result is a carefully calibrated and dynamic building that engenders an equally calibrated and dynamic educational environment.

TOP: Solarstudies of campus
BOTTOM: Site plan

OPPOSITE
TOP: Atrium view
BOTTOM: Exterior view

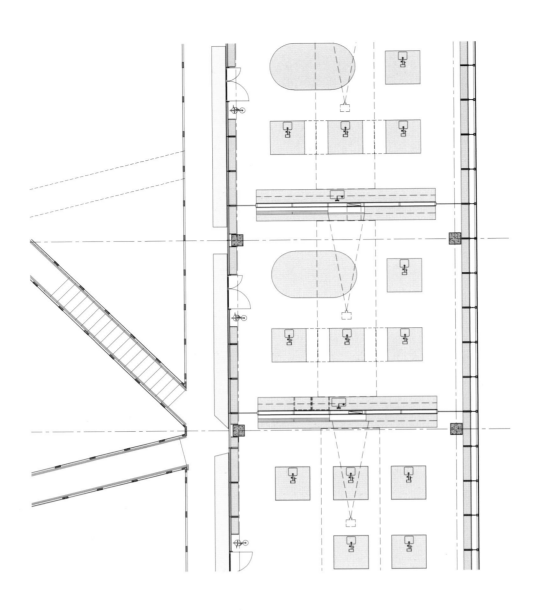

TOP: Enlarged typical lab
BOTTOM: Construction
sequence

OPPOSITE
TOP: View of bridges
BOTTOM: Section and plan

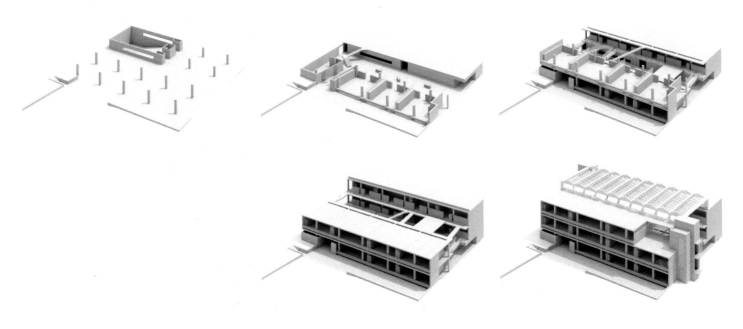

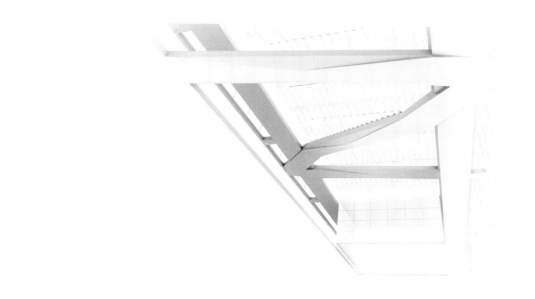

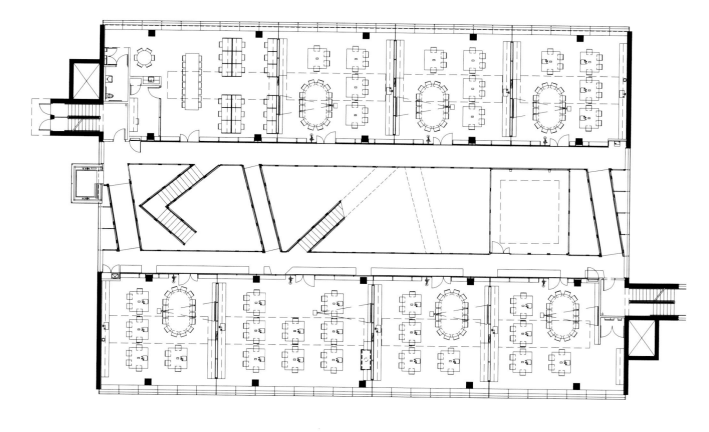

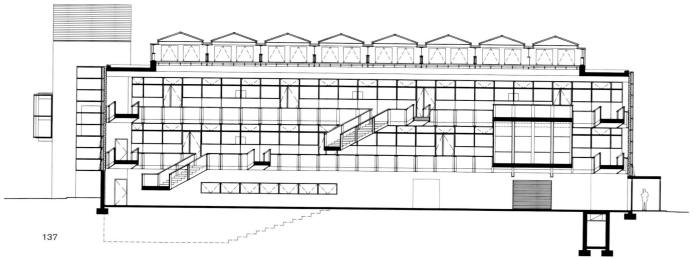

137

TOP: Perspective section
BOTTOM: Perspective section
with air flow

OPPOSITE
TOP: Atrium light studies
BOTTOM: Atrium view

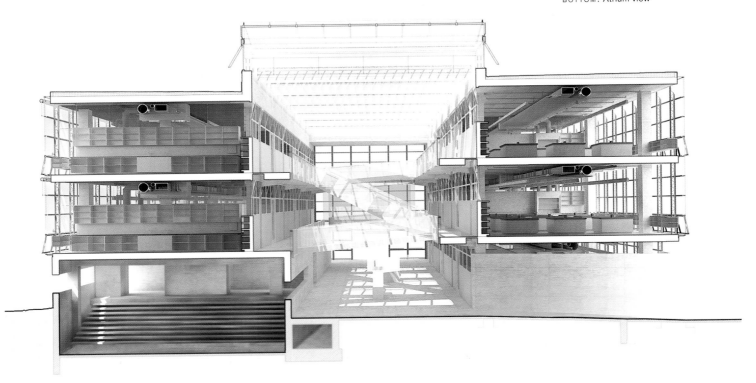

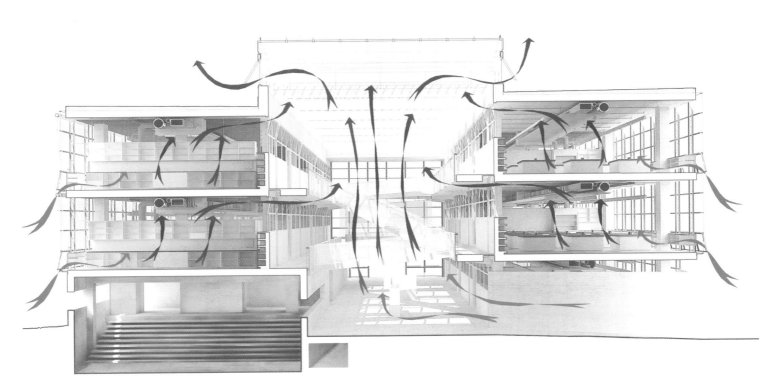

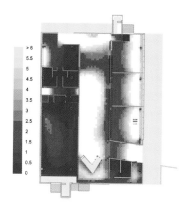
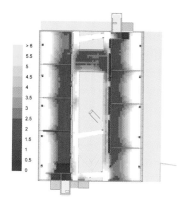
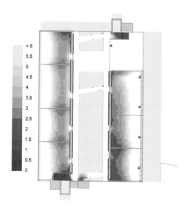

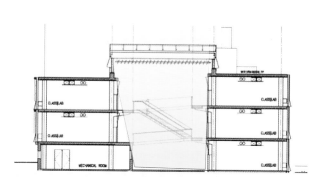
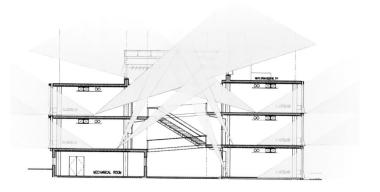

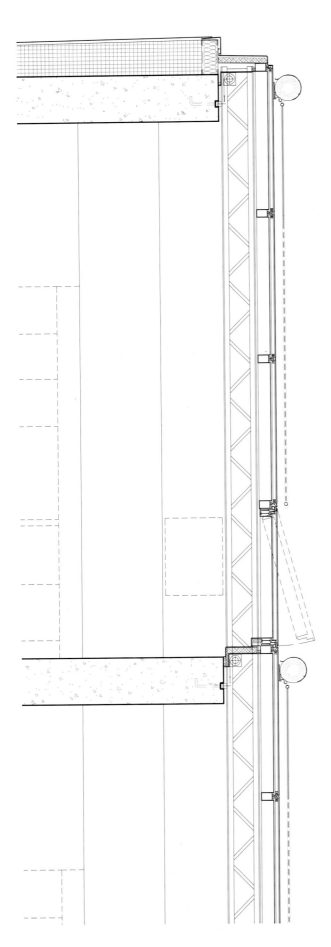

LEFT: Building envelope section

TOP RIGHT: Building envelope model view

BOTTOM RIGHT: Exterior view

OPPOSITE
TOP: Daylight study
BOTTOM: Laboratory section perspectives

140

# Interdisciplinary Science and Technology Building 2

Arizona State University, Tempe, Arizona

richärd+bauer Architecture, Phoenix, Arizona

**ARCHITECT:** richärd+bauer: Jim Richärd; Steve Kennedy, Associate Architect; Andrew Timberg, Project Architect/ Construction Administration
**STRUCTURAL ENGINEER:** Caruso, Turley, Scott: Richard Turley, John Thompson
**MECHANICAL AND PLUMBING ENGINEER:** Energy Systems Design: Monte Sturdevent
**LANDSCAPE ARCHITECT:** CF Schuler: Carol Schuler
**CIVIL ENGINEER:** KPFF: Jack Reeves
**LIGHTING:** Az Lighting
**SALES COST CONTROLLER:** CMCC, Contact: Adrianna Crnjac
**GENERAL CONTRACTOR:** Wespac Construction: Wayne Bogan, Sr., Project Manager
**CLIENT:** Arizona State University
**INTERIOR DESIGNER:** Kelly K. Bauer; Project Interior Designer: Stacey Kranz
**LAB PLANNER:** richärd + bauer, llc
**ELECTRICAL ENGINEER:** Energy Systems Designs: Kurt Longholtz
**LAB CONSULTANT:** ISEC: Steve Zediker
**PHOTOGRAPHER:** Bill Timmerman, Timmerman Photography

The 60,000-square-foot Interdisciplinary Science and Technology Building 2 at Arizona State University contains a large range of research agendas: soil dynamics, a river dynamics laboratory, structures testing labs, transportation planning, pavement research, geology, and the Sustainable Materials and Renewable Technology group. It is an incubator for engineering and science research on physical environments. Completed on a fast-track and low budget, the building is designed as a highly adaptable laboratory loft that can absorb varied research needs and serve to attract new faculty and research to the university.

A key morphological decision in the building, integrated design was to externalize the building circulation and mechanical systems in a central courtyard that runs the length of the building. This minimizes interior, conditioned construction square footage and greatly increases the serviceability of the structure. Evaporative cooling strategies in the 280-foot-long courtyard include water misters and large overhead fans. Courtyard evaporative cooling is a common climatic design feature in the southwest and is prevalent on the Arizona State University campus. Here the courtyard also accommodates fork-lift traffic. The courtyard is enclosed above by perforated Cor-Ten steel panels that modulate light and shade. This lowers the air temperature as much as twenty degrees in the Tempe summer. While the courtyard integrates technical and climatic systems, it also integrates the social systems of the building. The courtyard is punctuated in the upper floors by meeting space

conference rooms and "enclaves" that engender interaction amongst researchers, faculty, and students.

A service basement below the surface of the courtyard isolates major mechanical equipment and serves as the primary distribution zone for the building. Service troughs connect this basement to the high bay laboratory spaces that face the courtyard at grade. These twenty-two-foot-high spaces utilize floor-deep trusses to support the upper laboratory lofts. Each high bay space includes a mezzanine level for lab workstations, maximizing ground floor workspace. They are located opposite a clerestory window that provides daylight and views to the high bay lab and the workstations. The top floor, upper laboratory portion of the structure consists of laboratory lofts with demountable partitions that can shift with changing research agendas, funding, and research types. The research lofts have modular lab benches serviced by distribution troughs on each edge of the labs. There is a focus on quick adaptations to the lab configurations. Private and open office space for research support also occurs on this upper level.

The logic of its building systems and materials guides the expression of the building. The result is the exposure of its robust structure and surfaces. Economy and speed of construction were also critical factors that guided material decisions. The hollow-core precast concrete satisfied these requirements while also dampening vibrations that could otherwise affect laboratory equipment.

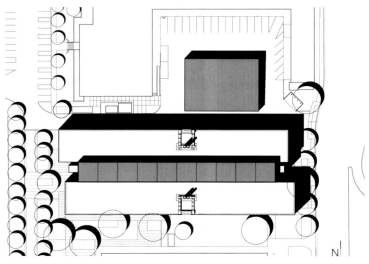

Site plan

OPPOSITE
West entry

INTERDISCIPLINARY
SCIENCE AND
TECHNOLOGY 2

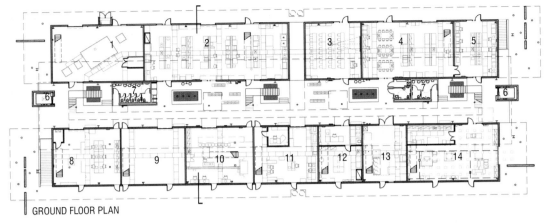

GROUND FLOOR PLAN

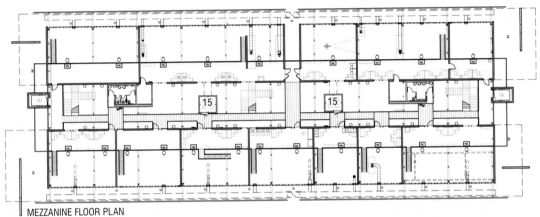

MEZZANINE FLOOR PLAN

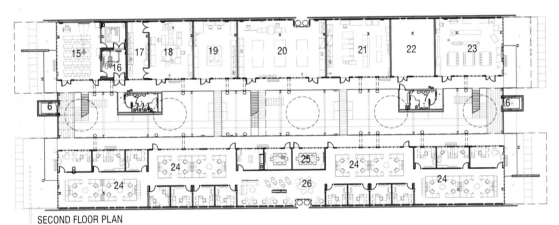

SECOND FLOOR PLAN

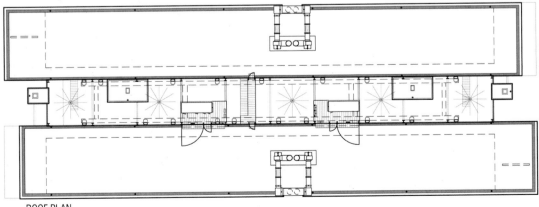

ROOF PLAN

OPPOSITE
TOP: Southeast view
BOTTOM: Entry view

GROUND FLOOR
1. SUPERSONIC WIND TUNNEL
2. PAVEMENT LAB
3. ORIENTATION LAB
4. SOILS TESTING LAB
5. ATM TESTING LAB
6. ELEVATOR
7. RESTROOM
8. FLUID DYNAMICS LAB
9. EXPANSION LAB
10. GEOGRAPHY LAB
11. MATERIALS TESTING LAB
12. MAE FLUID DYNAMICS LAB
13. EXPANSION LAB
14. STRUCTURE LAB

MEZZANINE
15. ENCLAVE

SECOND FLOOR
16. MAE CLASSROOM LAB
17. TURBINE/ICE TEST CELL
18. HEAT TRANSFER LAB
19. THERMODYNAMICS LAB
20. COMBUSTION RESEARCH
21. COMBUSTION LAB
22. EXPANSION LAB
23. HYDRAULICS LAB
24. OPEN/OFFICE SPACE
25. CONFERENCE ROOM
26. STUDY LOUNGE

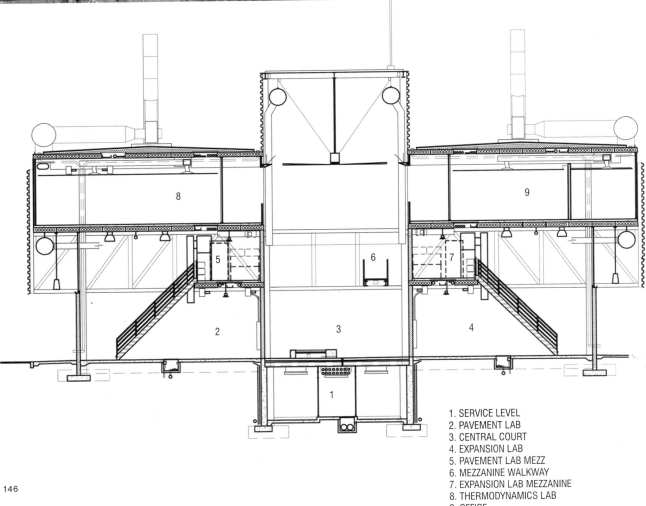

1. SERVICE LEVEL
2. PAVEMENT LAB
3. CENTRAL COURT
4. EXPANSION LAB
5. PAVEMENT LAB MEZZ
6. MEZZANINE WALKWAY
7. EXPANSION LAB MEZZANINE
8. THERMODYNAMICS LAB
9. OFFICE

# University of Arizona College of Architecture and Landscape Architecture

Tucson, Arizona

Jones Studio, Phoenix, Arizona

**ARCHITECT:** Jones Studio: Eddie Jones, Neal Jones,
Brian Farling, Maria Salenger
**STRUCTURAL ENGINEER:** Rudow + Berry: Mark Rudow,
Keith Berry
**MECHANICAL AND PLUMBING ENGINEER:** Kunka Engineering:
Pete Kunka
**ELECTRICAL ENGINEER:** Woodward Engineering:
Doug Woodward
**LANDSCAPE ARCHITECT:** Ten Eyck: Christy Ten Eyck,
Todd Briggs
**CIVIL ENGINEER:** Evans Kuhn & Associates: John Gray
**ACOUSTICAL:** McKay Conant Brook: Dave Conant
**GENERAL CONTRACTOR:** Lloyd Construction
**U OF A COLLEGE OF ARCHITECTURE AND LANDSCAPE
ARCHITECTURE:** Dean Richard Eribes, Dean Chuck
Albanese, CALA Design Advisory Board
**U OF A FACILITIES DESIGN AND CONSTRUCTION:**
Debra Johnson, May Carr, Rick Marsh

This renovation and addition project at the University of Arizona College of Architecture and Landscape Architecture is intended to foster collaboration amongst its disciplines through its programming and physical systems. The project consists of the renovation of an existing architecture building and the addition of an equal-size building with new collaborative studios, seminar space, and a materials lab. This will allow the landscape architecture department to join the architecture department in a single facility. The insertions and excavations in the site lyrically and literally integrate the two departments, as well as the college, with the university campus through construction, landscape, air, light, and water strategies.

For the 33,000-square-foot new construction, the architects inserted a long bar on the north side of the site, creating a tree canopy-shaded courtyard pool and exterior instruction space on the south. This configuration provides excellent northern light and allows every occupiable space to be day lit. The open studios are zoned against the north wall, while classroom and office spaces are on the south side of the new construction. The south side of the building is an eight-foot-deep zone with a screen-faced wall of vines, which are an extension of the courtyard plantings below and form the primary solar-control system for the addition. This will yield dappled light and shade for the space beyond once the vegetation matures. The east and west walls are solid, blocking heat gains from these unfavorable orientations. Other strategies for minimizing energy consumption include exterior vertical circulation and a roof structured to engender photovoltaic, solar hot water, wind turbine, and vegetated roof experiments, which

align with the research ambitions of the school. All exterior balconies are oversized, maximizing social opportunities outside during the temperate school-year climate. The top-floor seminar room, common office spaces, and design jury rooms have sliding glass doors that open to balconies behind the vegetated screen wall and allow fresh air into these spaces. The materials lab and shop at grade has ten garage doors that open to allow air and student work in the labs to cross the boundary of the building.

A central aspect of the project is the harvesting of water for the courtyard landscape irrigation. Four water systems feed a centralized harvesting tank and, ultimately, the irrigated landscape courtyard and outdoor classroom. Gray water, cooling-tower condensation, and roof stormwater collected in a single gutter, draining to a centralized forty-two-foot-tall, seven and a half feet in diameter 11,500-gallon fiberglass storage tank. Blow-off water from an adjacent campus well-water-pumping station is sent directly to a constructed riparian demonstration garden. The system demonstrates resourceful relationships between landscape and building for the college.

The new building was detailed with sparse construction systems and exposed connections that are didactically in view for students. Supply and return ducts are also available for student observation. There is an emphasis on materials that will weather in the climate and require minimal maintenance. As such, in all cases the architects seek ambitious effects with modest resources.

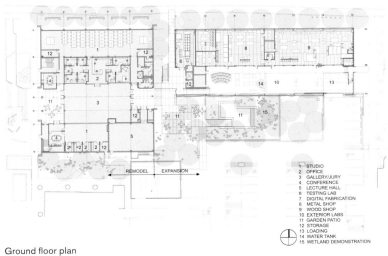

Ground floor plan

OPPOSITE
TOP: Corner view of new building
BOTTOM: Detail views

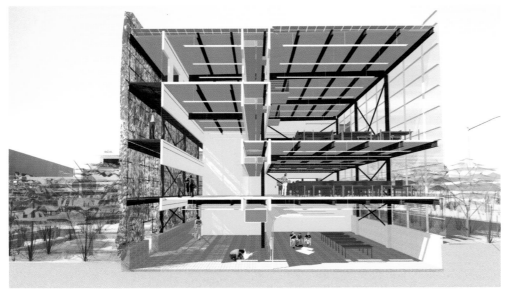

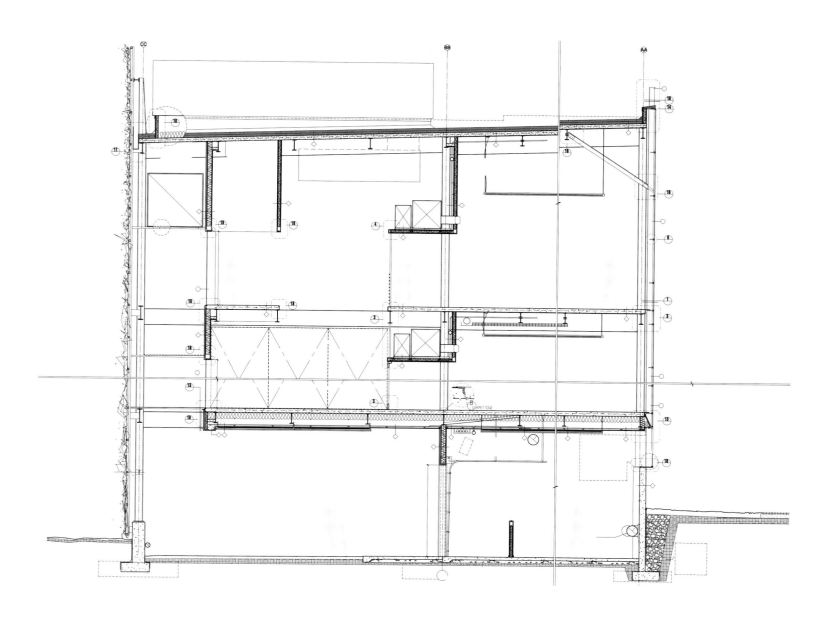

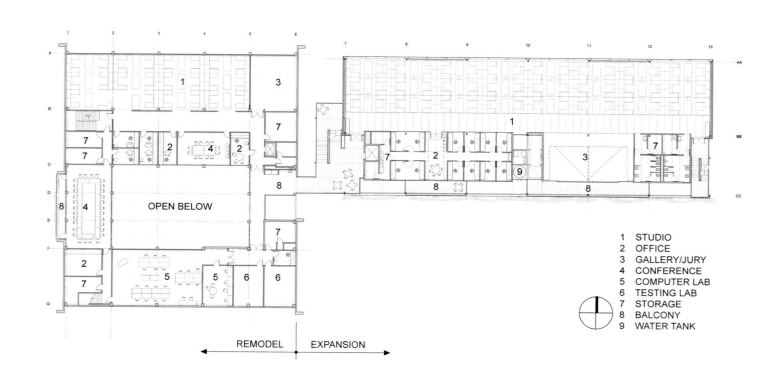

1 STUDIO
2 OFFICE
3 GALLERY/JURY
4 CONFERENCE
5 COMPUTER LAB
6 TESTING LAB
7 STORAGE
8 BALCONY
9 WATER TANK

OPEN BELOW

REMODEL     EXPANSION

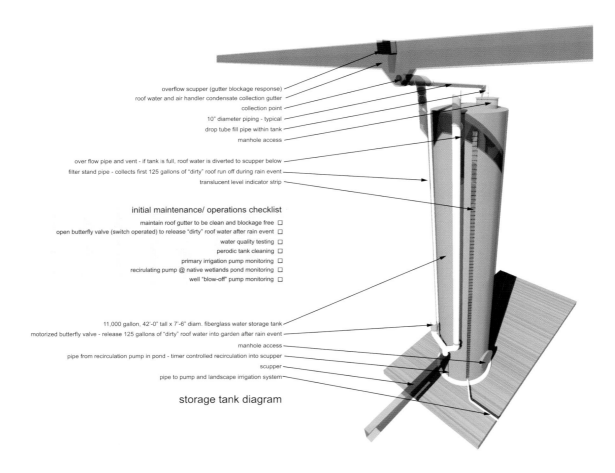

overflow scupper (gutter blockage response)
roof water and air handler condensate collection gutter
collection point
10" diameter piping - typical
drop tube fill pipe within tank
manhole access

over flow pipe and vent - if tank is full, roof water is diverted to scupper below
filter stand pipe - collects first 125 gallons of "dirty" roof run off during rain event
translucent level indicator strip

### initial maintenance/ operations checklist

maintain roof gutter to be clean and blockage free ☐
open butterfly valve (switch operated) to release "dirty" roof water after rain event ☐
water quality testing ☐
perodic tank cleaning ☐
primary irrigation pump monitoring ☐
recirulating pump @ native wetlands pond monitoring ☐
well "blow-off" pump monitoring ☐

11,000 gallon, 42'-0" tall x 7'-6" diam. fiberglass water storage tank
motorized butterfly valve - release 125 gallons of "dirty" roof water into garden after rain event
manhole access
pipe from recirculation pump in pond - timer controlled recirculation into scupper
scupper
pipe to pump and landscape irrigation system

### storage tank diagram

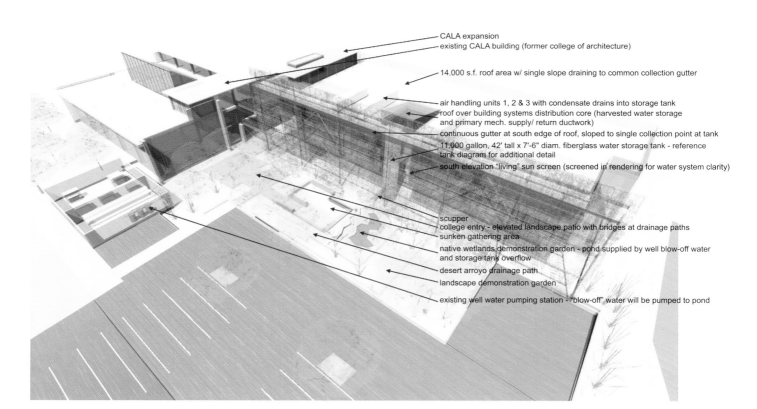

CALA expansion
existing CALA building (former college of architecture)

14,000 s.f. roof area w/ single slope draining to common collection gutter

air handling units 1, 2 & 3 with condensate drains into storage tank
roof over building systems distribution core (harvested water storage
and primary mech. supply/ return ductwork)
continuous gutter at south edge of roof, sloped to single collection point at tank
11,000 gallon, 42' tall x 7'-6" diam. fiberglass water storage tank - reference
tank diagram for additional detail
south elevation "living" sun screen (screened in rendering for water system clarity)

scupper
college entry - elevated landscape patio with bridges at drainage paths
sunken gathering area
native wetlands demonstration garden - pond supplied by well blow-off water
and storage tank overflow
desert arroyo drainage path
landscape demonstration garden
existing well water pumping station - "blow-off" water will be pumped to pond

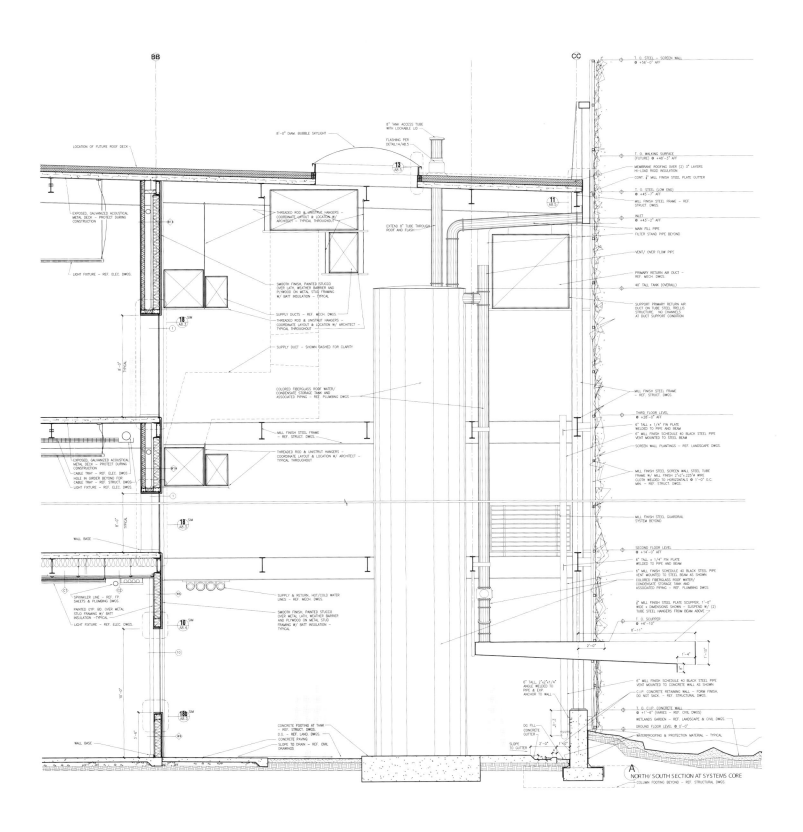

BB

CC

8'-0" DIAM. BUBBLE SKYLIGHT

8" TANK ACCESS TUBE
WITH LOCKABLE LID

FLASHING PER
DETAIL 14/A8.5

T. O. STEEL - SCREEN WALL
@ +56'-0" AFF

LOCATION OF FUTURE ROOF DECK

T. O. WALKING SURFACE
(FUTURE) @ +48'-3" AFF

MEMBRANE ROOFING OVER (2) 3" LAYERS
HI-LOAD RIGID INSULATION

CONT. ⅜" MILL FINISH STEEL PLATE GUTTER

T. O. STEEL (LOW END)
@ +45'-7" AFF

MILL FINISH STEEL FRAME - REF.
STRUCT. DWGS.

EXPOSED, GALVANIZED ACOUSTICAL
METAL DECK - PROTECT DURING
CONSTRUCTION

THREADED ROD & UNISTRUT HANGERS -
COORDINATE LAYOUT & LOCATION W/
ARCHITECT - TYPICAL THROUGHOUT

EXTEND 8" TUBE THROUGH
ROOF AND FLASH

INLET
@ +43'-2" AFF

MAIN FILL PIPE

FILTER STAND PIPE BEYOND

VENT/ OVER FLOW PIPE

LIGHT FIXTURE - REF. ELEC. DWGS.

PRIMARY RETURN AIR DUCT -
REF. MECH. DWGS.

40' TALL TANK (OVERALL)

SMOOTH FINISH, PAINTED STUCCO
OVER LATH, WEATHER BARRIER AND
PLYWOOD ON METAL STUD FRAMING
W/ BATT INSULATION - TYPICAL

SUPPORT PRIMARY RETURN AIR
DUCT ON TUBE STEEL TRELLIS
STRUCTURE. NO CHANNELS
AT DUCT SUPPORT CONDITION

SUPPLY DUCTS - REF. MECH. DWGS.

THREADED ROD & UNISTRUT HANGERS -
COORDINATE LAYOUT & LOCATION W/ ARCHITECT -
TYPICAL THROUGHOUT

18 SIM
A8.3

SUPPLY DUCT - SHOWN DASHED FOR CLARITY

COLORED FIBERGLASS ROOF WATER/
CONDENSATE STORAGE TANK AND
ASSOCIATED PIPING - REF. PLUMBING DWGS.

MILL FINISH STEEL FRAME
- REF. STRUCT. DWGS.

THIRD FLOOR LEVEL
@ +28'-0" AFF

6" TALL x ¼" FIN PLATE
WELDED TO PIPE AND BEAM

EXPOSED, GALVANIZED ACOUSTICAL
METAL DECK - PROTECT DURING
CONSTRUCTION

MILL FINISH STEEL FRAME
- REF. STRUCT. DWGS.

6" MILL FINISH SCHEDULE 40 BLACK STEEL PIPE
VENT MOUNTED TO STEEL BEAM

CABLE TRAY - REF. ELEC. DWGS.

THREADED ROD & UNISTRUT HANGERS -
COORDINATE LAYOUT & LOCATION W/ ARCHITECT -
TYPICAL THROUGHOUT

SCREEN WALL PLANTINGS - REF. LANDSCAPE DWGS.

HOLE IN GIRDER BEYOND FOR
CABLE TRAY - REF. STRUCT. DWGS.

LIGHT FIXTURE - REF. ELEC. DWGS.

MILL FINISH STEEL SCREEN WALL STEEL TUBE
FRAME W/ MILL FINISH 2"x2"x.225"Ø WIRE
CLOTH WELDED TO HORIZONTALS @ 1'-0" O.C.
MIN. - REF. STRUCT. DWGS.

18 SIM
A8.3

MILL FINISH STEEL GUARDRAIL
SYSTEM BEYOND

WALL BASE

SECOND FLOOR LEVEL
@ +14'-0" AFF

6" TALL x ¼" FIN PLATE
WELDED TO PIPE AND BEAM

6" MILL FINISH SCHEDULE 40 BLACK STEEL PIPE
VENT MOUNTED TO STEEL BEAM AS SHOWN

SPRINKLER LINE - REF. F.P.
SHEETS & PLUMBING DWGS.

SUPPLY & RETURN, HOT/COLD WATER
LINES - REF. MECH. DWGS.

COLORED FIBERGLASS ROOF WATER/
CONDENSATE STORAGE TANK AND
ASSOCIATED PIPING - REF. PLUMBING DWGS.

PAINTED GYP. BD. OVER METAL
STUD FRAMING W/ BATT
INSULATION - TYPICAL

SMOOTH FINISH, PAINTED STUCCO
OVER METAL LATH, WEATHER BARRIER AND
PLYWOOD ON METAL STUD
FRAMING W/ BATT INSULATION -
TYPICAL

⅜" MILL FINISH STEEL PLATE SCUPPER, 1'-0"
WIDE x DIMENSIONS SHOWN - SUSPEND W/ (2)
TUBE STEEL HANGERS FROM BEAM ABOVE

10 SIM
A8.4

T. O. SCUPPER
@ +6'-10"

8'-11"

2'-0"

1'-4"

10 SIM
A8.3

6" TALL 2"x2"x¼"
ANGLE WELDED TO
PIPE & EXP
ANCHOR TO WALL

6" MILL FINISH SCHEDULE 40 BLACK STEEL PIPE
VENT MOUNTED TO CONCRETE WALL AS SHOWN

C.I.P. CONCRETE RETAINING WALL - FORM FINISH,
DO NOT SACK - REF. STRUCTURAL DWGS.

T. O. C.I.P. CONCRETE WALL
@ +1'-6" (VARIES - REF. CIVIL DWGS)

WETLANDS GARDEN - REF. LANDSCAPE & CIVIL DWGS.

GROUND FLOOR LEVEL
@ 0'-0"

WALL BASE

CONCRETE FOOTING AT TANK -
REF. STRUCT. DWGS.

D.G. - REF. LAND. DWGS.

SLOPE TO DRAIN - REF. CIVIL
DRAWINGS

DG FILL

CONCRETE
GUTTER

SLOPE
TO GUTTER

WATERPROOFING & PROTECTION MATERIAL - TYPICAL

A
NORTH/ SOUTH SECTION AT SYSTEMS CORE

COLUMN FOOTING BEYOND - REF. STRUCTURAL DWGS.

# Sidwell Friends School Middle School Renovation and Addition

Washington, D.C.

———

## KieranTimberlake Associates

**ARCHITECT:** KieranTimberlake Associates: Stephen Kieran, Design Partner; James Timberlake, Design Partner; Richard Hodge, Project Manager; Amy Floresta, Project Manager; Casey Boss, Project Architect; Sam Robinson, Project Architect; Project Team: Steven Johns, Jeff Goldstein, Snezana Litvinovic, Benita Lee, Paul Worrell, Marceli Botticelli, Gavin Riggall, Isaiah King, Jonathan Ferrari, Seth Trance, Gabriel Biller, Tricia Stuth, Rod Bates, Karl Wallick, Richard Seltenrich, Nick Wallin, Brian Carney
**STRUCTURAL ENGINEER:** CVM Structural Engineers
**MECHANICAL, ELECTRICAL, AND PLUMBING ENGINEER:** Bruce E. Brooks and Associates
**LANDSCAPE ARCHITECT:** Andropogon
**CIVIL ENGINEER:** VIKA
**LIGHTING:** Sean O'Connor Associates Lighting Consultants, and Benya Lighting Design
**ACOUSTICAL:** Shen Milsom and Wilke
**INTERIOR DESIGNER:** KieranTimberlake Associates
**WETLAND CONSULTANT:** Natural Systems International
**SUSTAINABLE DESIGN CONSULTANTS:** GreenShape and Integrative Design Collaborative
**EXTERIOR ENVELOPE CONSULTANTS:** Simpson Gumpertz and Heger
**INFORMATION DISPLAY CONSULTANT:** Lucid Design Group
**GENERAL CONTRACTOR:** HITT Contracting
This project is LEED Platinum certified.

The 70,000-square-foot Sidwell Friends Middle School Addition and Renovation project in Washington, D.C., integrates an outmoded instructional facility, new instruction spaces, a teaching garden, and the energy available on its site. The landscape is the primary capture and channel device in the project. It collects people, light, and water as interconnected systems. Vegetated roofs collect, filter, and direct stormwater to a cistern and channel it to a biology pond that will host native species. Gray water from the building is also collected, treated, and then channeled through the small constructed wetland. This wetland decomposes microorganisms from the building gray water as it courses through the terraced configuration, responding to the site topography. The vegetated roof also functions as a container garden for students and roof-mounted photovoltaic panels will also be visible. The panels will supply about 5 percent of the building's electricity. There is a deliberate attempt to make these systems visible to the students where possible.

The building, the site, and their systems are organized by the path of the sun, seen here as the primary source of energy for the project. The building maximizes daylight while minimizing solar gain with the metal, horizontal solar-control devices and vertical wood solar-control cladding systems facing the landscape. The western red cedar wood for the solar-control system is reclaimed from one hundred-year-old wine casks and was designed and fabricated off-site as integrated panels. These vertical wood slats face the building's eastern and western exposures. The south-facing solar-control devices are horizontal and optimize solar shading.

Solar chimneys punctuate the roof line of the new construction. South-facing glazing at the top of the solar chimney heats up the surface and air of the chimney. The chimneys induce air flow through the classroom spaces with cooler air, from the north side of the new building, drawn to the chimneys by the heated air. The chimneys are designed to work in both power and nonpower operated modes. The narrow dimension of the single loaded floor plate works well for both the ventilation and daylighting of the classrooms. A series of light shelves line the south-facing corridor and bounce light toward the north-facing classrooms. The result is ample, diffused light for the classroom spaces.

Throughout the project the various integrated systems are didactically exposed and presented as an educational implement. The building's systems constantly make connections between local, immediate phenomenon and regional and global phenomena. The school sees numerous ways to integrate the building's performance with its curriculum, sensitizing the students and perhaps affecting their decisions as future citizens and policy makers.

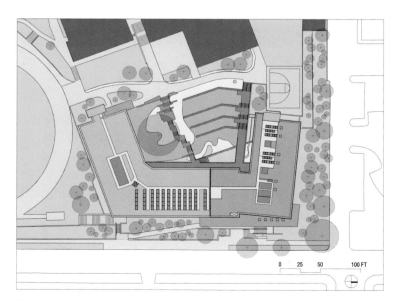

0   25   50   100 FT

Site plan

OPPOSITE
Entry view

TOP: Solar control
BOTTOM: Solar-control panel
types

OPPOSITE
TOP: Plans
BOTTOM: Eastern view

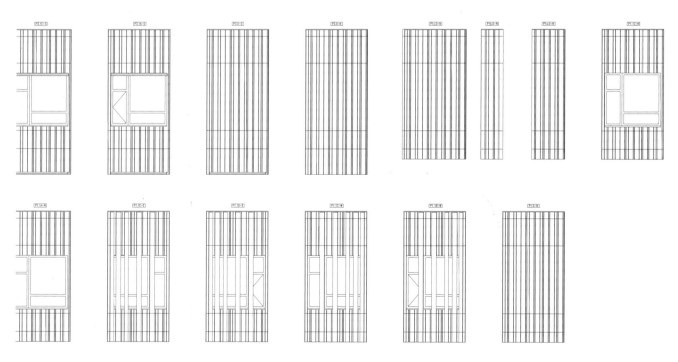

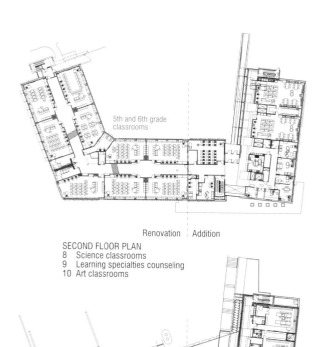

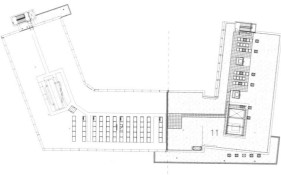

5th and 6th grade classrooms

Renovation | Addition

SECOND FLOOR PLAN
8   Science classrooms
9   Learning specialties counseling
10  Art classrooms

Renovation | Addition

ROOF PLAN
11  Planted roof
12  Photovoltaic panels

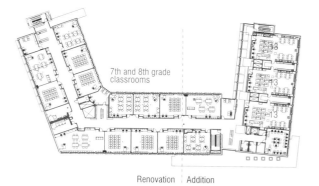

7th and 8th grade classrooms

Renovation | Addition

FIRST FLOOR PLAN
1   Lobby              5   Drama
2   Administrative offce   6   Choral music
3   Art classrooms     7   Instrumental music
4   Library

Renovation | Addition

THIRD FLOOR PLAN
13  Science Classrooms

N

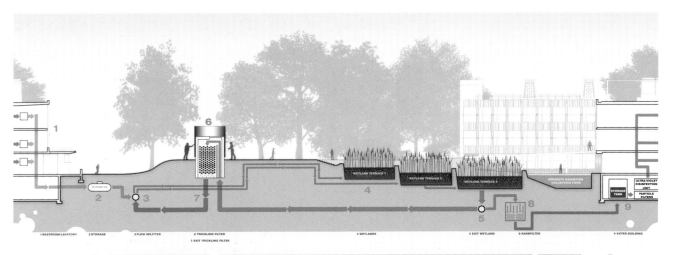

**WASTE WATER TREATMENT SYSTEM**

1 RESTROOM/LAVATORY    2 STORAGE    3 FLOW SPLITTER    6 TRICKLING FILTER    4 WETLANDS    5 EXIT WETLAND    8 SANDFILTER    9 ENTER BUILDING

7 EXIT TRICKLING FILTER

TOP: Water retention and
treatment diagram
BOTTOM: Building capturing
water, people, light, and air

OPPOSITE
TOP: Water filtration diagram
BOTTOM: Courtyard view

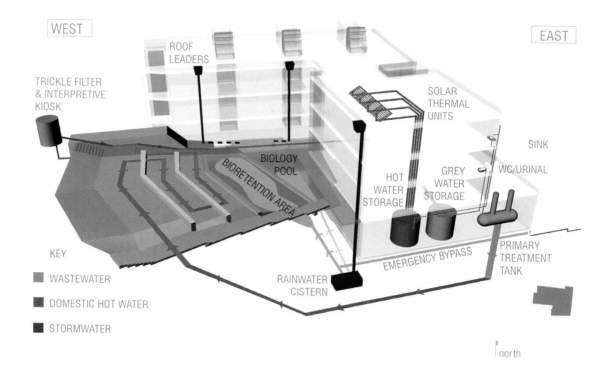

WEST

EAST

ROOF
LEADERS

TRICKLE FILTER
& INTERPRETIVE
KIOSK

SOLAR
THERMAL
UNITS

SINK

BIOLOGY
POOL

WC/URINAL

BIORETENTION AREA

HOT
WATER
STORAGE

GREY
WATER
STORAGE

KEY

RAINWATER
CISTERN

EMERGENCY BYPASS

PRIMARY
TREATMENT
TANK

██ WASTEWATER

██ DOMESTIC HOT WATER

██ STORMWATER

north

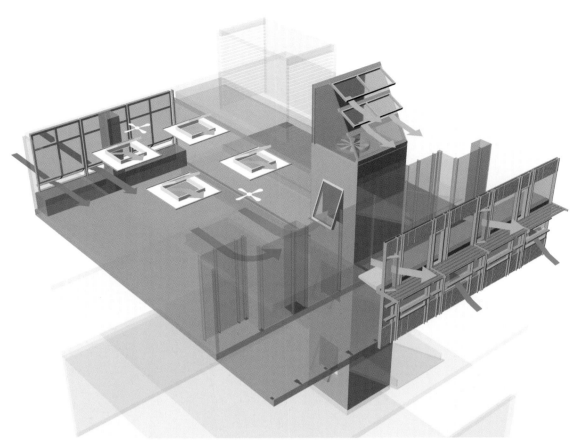

NORTH-SOUTH SECTION THROUGH
ADDITION LOOKING EAST

EAST-WEST SECTION THROUGH ADDITION LOOKING EAST

# Technology Access Foundation, White Center

Lakewood, Washington

Miller|Hull Partnership, Seattle, Washington

**ARCHITECTURAL TEAM:** Miller|Hull Partnership: Craig
Curtis, Design Partner; Evan Bourquard, Project Architect;
Caroline Kreiser, Project Manager
**STRUCTURAL ENGINEER:** Bright Engineering
**MECHANICAL AND ACOUSTICAL ENGINEER:** The Greenbusch
Group
**ELECTRICAL ENGINEER:** CB Engineers
**CIVIL AND LANDSCAPE ENGINEER:** SvR Design Company
**SALVAGE/BRANDING:** Public Architecture
**INTERIORS:** 33 Design Company

The 24,000-square-foot Community Learning Center
for the Technology Access Foundation (TAF) is an
administration and technology education center that uses
in-house computer labs and facilities in local schools to
provide technology-based training for children in Seattle's
most economically challenged and racially diverse
neighborhoods. The mission is to prepare these students
for higher education and professional work with skills
relevant to the twenty-first century. The Community Learning
Center will also function as a community center for the
Lakewood Park area in King County. The building contains
offices on its upper floors, the technology center on the
main floor, and a community center and kitchen on the first
floor. The program organization anticipates multiple renting
scenarios in order to provide a spatially and economically
adaptable building for the TAF organization and the county.

King County donated property within Lakewood Park for
the project. In order to respect the existing park landscape,
the aim was to minimize disruption to the site with the
building and its construction. The morphology of the
building is determined by site conditions. All existing healthy
trees were preserved on the site. The building is positioned
close to these existing trees for desirable shading and
experiential qualities. Access to adjacent parking and
access to views determine the asymmetrical V configuration
of the building. To reduce parking and encourage low or
no emission modes of transportation, the building provides
ample bicycle parking, showers, and preferred parking for
low-emission vehicles.

The building is a steel and glass box with various
enclosing, repurposed cladding materials in discrete
portions of the building envelope. Miller|Hull worked with
Public Architecture in San Francisco to help identify locally
salvaged materials for use throughout the building. The
strategy reduces material costs, redirects material flow from
landfills, and capitalizes on material and labor donations for
the nonprofit organization. Examples include repurposed
steel scraps on the main circulation stairs, metal shop off-

cuts used as exterior cladding shingles applied as a rainscreen system, solid-core doors reused as wall paneling,
fire hose partitions in the offices, and salvaged wood for an
approach bridge.

The steel and glass box provides ample daylight for
the offices and technology classrooms. Operable glazing
throughout the building will facilitate cross-ventilation
strategies on the main floor and buoyant air strategies on
the office floor with rooftop vents. Mechanical rooms are
decentralized around the classroom floor plan to reduce
duct runs and improve efficiency. They feed intake air into a
raised floor plenum for displacement ventilation. The office
floor uses a hydronic concrete slab for heating and cooling.
The same floor also utilizes a hydronic chilled beam for
additional cooling during peak temperatures. As with other
nonprofit institutions, the building's integrated strategies
serve to lower operating costs, directing funding toward
its mission rather than operating costs.

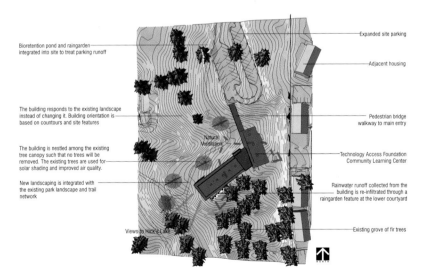

Bioretention pond and raingarden integrated into site to treat parking runoff

Expanded site parking

Adjacent housing

The building responds to the existing landscape instead of changing it. Building orientation is based on countours and site features

Pedestrian bridge walkway to main entry

Natural Ventilation

The building is nestled among the existing tree canopy such that no trees will be removed. The existing trees are used for solar shading and improved air quality

Technology Access Foundation Community Learning Center

New landscaping is integrated with the existing park landscape and trail network

Rainwater runoff collected from the building is re-infiltrated through a raingarden feature at the lower courtyard

Views to Hick's Lake

Existing grove of fir trees

Site plan

OPPOSITE
TOP: Exterior view from park
BOTTOM: Entry view

163

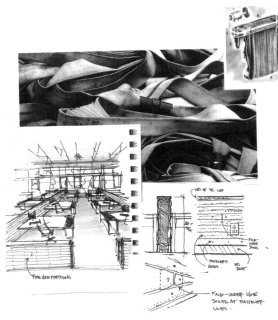

are you **TAF** material?

6.14.06

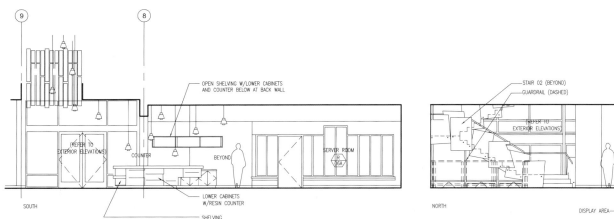

OPEN SHELVING W/LOWER CABINETS
AND COUNTER BELOW AT BACK WALL

(REFER TO
EXTERIOR ELEVATIONS)

COUNTER          BEYOND

SERVER ROOM
R
06A

SOUTH

LOWER CABINETS
W/RESIN COUNTER

SHELVING

STAIR 02 (BEYOND)
GUARDRAIL (DASHED)

(REFER TO
EXTERIOR ELEVATIONS)

(REFER TO
EXTERIOR ELEVATIONS)

NORTH

DISPLAY AREA

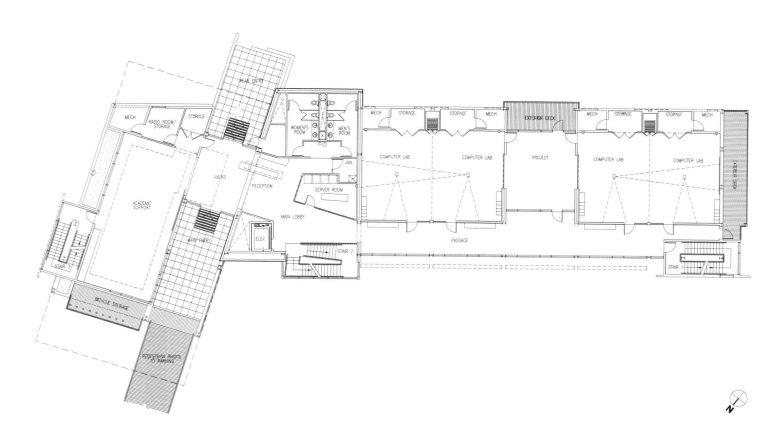

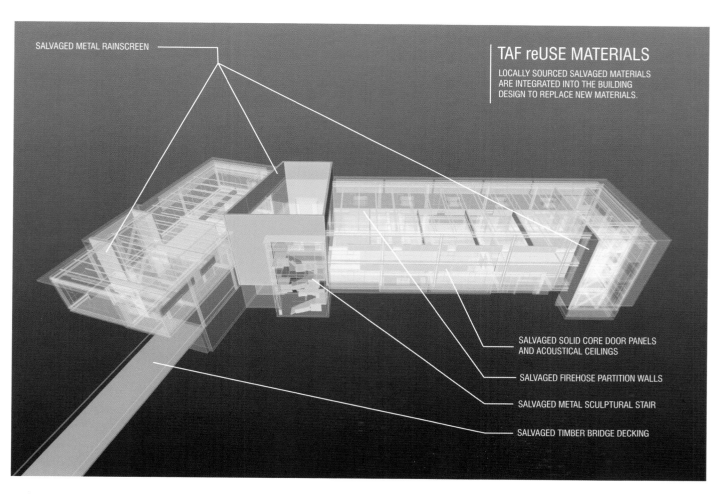

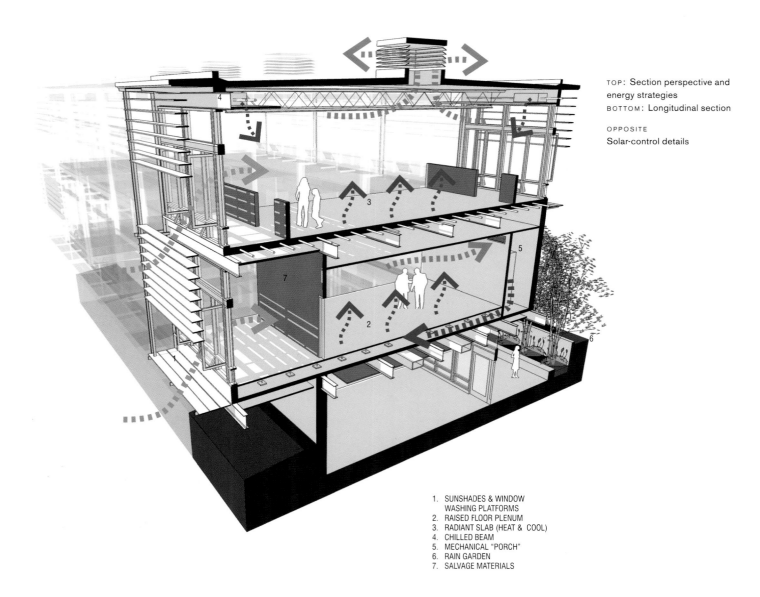

1. SUNSHADES & WINDOW
   WASHING PLATFORMS
2. RAISED FLOOR PLENUM
3. RADIANT SLAB (HEAT & COOL)
4. CHILLED BEAM
5. MECHANICAL "PORCH"
6. RAIN GARDEN
7. SALVAGE MATERIALS

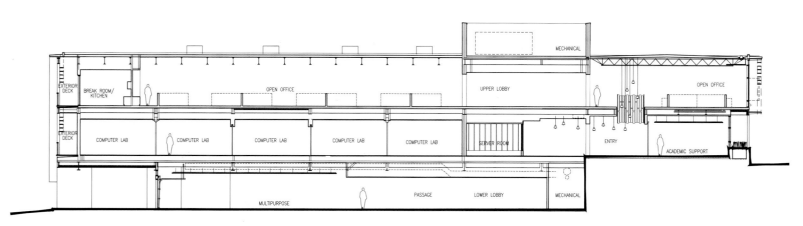

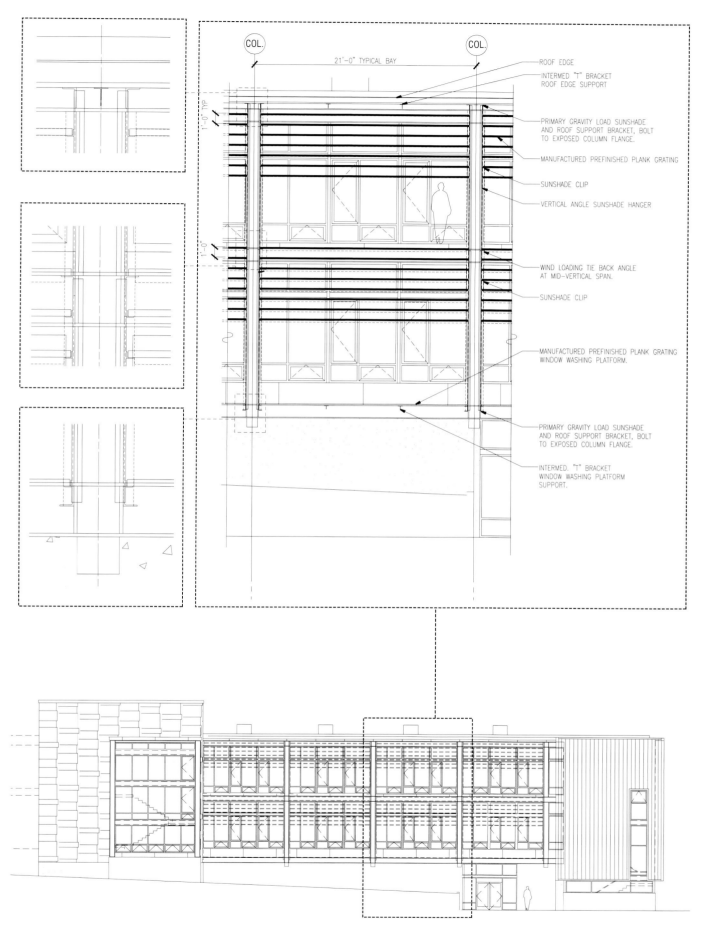

COL.

COL.

21'-0" TYPICAL BAY

ROOF EDGE

INTERMED "T" BRACKET
ROOF EDGE SUPPORT

PRIMARY GRAVITY LOAD SUNSHADE
AND ROOF SUPPORT BRACKET, BOLT
TO EXPOSED COLUMN FLANGE.

MANUFACTURED PREFINISHED PLANK GRATING

SUNSHADE CLIP

VERTICAL ANGLE SUNSHADE HANGER

WIND LOADING TIE BACK ANGLE
AT MID-VERTICAL SPAN.

SUNSHADE CLIP

MANUFACTURED PREFINISHED PLANK GRATING
WINDOW WASHING PLATFORM.

PRIMARY GRAVITY LOAD SUNSHADE
AND ROOF SUPPORT BRACKET, BOLT
TO EXPOSED COLUMN FLANGE.

INTERMED. "T" BRACKET
WINDOW WASHING PLATFORM
SUPPORT.

1'-0 TYP

1'-0

# Artists for Humanity EpiCenter

Boston, Massachusetts

---

Arrowstreet, Somerville, Massachusetts

**ARCHITECT:** Arrowstreet: James Batchelor, Pat Cornelison
**STRUCTURAL ENGINEER:** Rene Mugnier Associates: Rene Mugnier
**MECHANICAL ENGINEER:** Zade Company: Mohammed Zade
**CIVIL ENGINEER:** Samiotes Consultants: Steve Garvin
**CONTRACTOR:** T.R. White Company: David Marceau
**LIGHTING DESIGNER:** US Lighting Consultants: Addison Kelly
**ENVIRONMENTAL BUILDING CONSULTANT:** Building Science Engineering: Mark Kelley
**ARTIST:** Nick Rodrigues
**COMMISSIONING AGENT:** Shooshanian Engineering; Michael Kjelgaard
**OWNER/DEVELOPER:** Artists for Humanity: Susan Rodgerson
This project is LEED Platinum certified.

The mission of the Artists for Humanity EpiCenter is "to bridge economic, racial, and social divisions by providing underserved youth with the keys to self-sufficiency through paid employment in the arts." This combination of social optimism and economic realism is evident in their recently completed EpiCenter building. The 23,500-square-foot facility combines a large gallery and reception space, various studios, and administrative space on a tight budget. The integration of construction and energy systems is an extension of the mission but it is also a sound model for a nonprofit. The low-energy building lowers operational costs, directing funding toward its programs.

The straightforward composition of the building is organized around several large, open, program spaces, integrating programmatic planning with energy and construction strategies. The north-south orientation of the building provides good solar orientation for its glazed short facades. Large floor-to-floor heights allow maximal daylight and direct solar gain in the unobstructed gallery and studio spaces. Fluorescent T-8 fixtures with light and occupancy sensors further minimize electrical loads.

The section prioritizes solar orientation and zoning in its disposition. A 42-kilowatt photovoltaic array is designed as a single surface mounted on the roof, engendering self-cleaning, to some degree, and shading the roof surface, minimizing heat gain. The pitch of the roof to the south generates a space for a mechanical mezzanine within the building's section, integrating equipment that might otherwise be on the roof where they would cast shadows on the photovoltaic panels. The roof slope also collects rainwater, which is harvested to irrigate a modest courtyard landscape. Material choices emphasize durability and recycled or repurposed content. Several salvaged materials were reused in the building, such as the automobile windshields that function as guardrails, and railroad tracks that function as the structure for exterior guardrails.

There is no refrigerant-based air conditioning in the building, eliminating 275,000 kilowatt-hours of electricity. The cooling strategies focus upon eliminating heat loads with a highly insulated building envelope and optimized use of daylight and efficient lamp fixtures. At night, operable windows are open and a whole-building fan evacuates hot air that accumulates each day, drawing the air through a central ventilation shaft. Each morning the windows are shut to retain the cool night air. On hot days, the ventilation shaft and large fan can be used to exchange air more rapidly, along with ceiling fans. The large, unobstructed program zones facilitate this ventilation strategy.

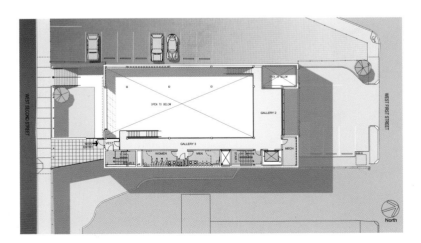

Mezzanine plan and site

OPPOSITE
TOP: EpiCenter context
BOTTOM: Northern view

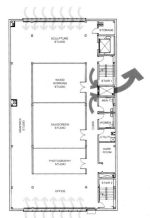

**TYPICAL STUDIO FLOOR**
Night-time Purge
At the end of the day when the occupants leave, the windows are opened and the summer vent exhausts all the air from the building. The windows are closed in the early morning to retain the cooler air and the ceiling fans are run for localized cooling. At the point that the inside air is as warm as the outside air, the summer vent can be turned on to force air through the building.

**TYPICAL STUDIO FLOOR**
Natural Ventilation with Ceiling Fan Recirculation
The windows are opened for natural ventilation during temperate weather. Individually controlled fans provide additional air movement. Dedicated exhaust removes undesirable fumes.

**TYPICAL STUDIO FLOOR**
Mechanical Ventilation with Dedicated Exhaust
During winter weather, the recirculated and heat-recovered air provides ventilation and dedicated exhaust removes undesirable fumes. (Ceiling fans can also be used for destratification.)

Energy strategies for studios and gallery

OPPOSITE
TOP: Section and energy diagram
BOTTOM: Upper studio view

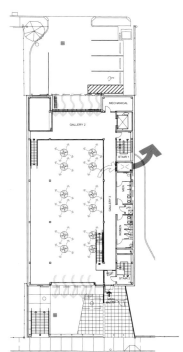

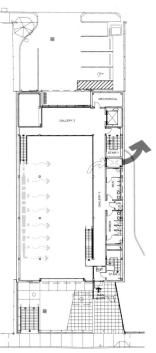

**GALLERY AND MEZZANINE**
Natural Ventilation with Ceiling Fan Recirculation
Gallery can be naturally ventilated from operable windows and 24' x 18' roll-up door to the gallery courtyard. The ceiling fans can be used to circulate gallery air and the summer vent can be run to force air in from both ends of the building.

**GALLERY AND MEZZANINE**
Dedicated Event Ventilation with Supplemental Exhaust through Summer Vent Shaft
During large gallery events a dedicated ventilation air-handling unit starts to provide tempered fresh air to the gallery. Summer vent can be optionally used to remove hot air from the gallery.

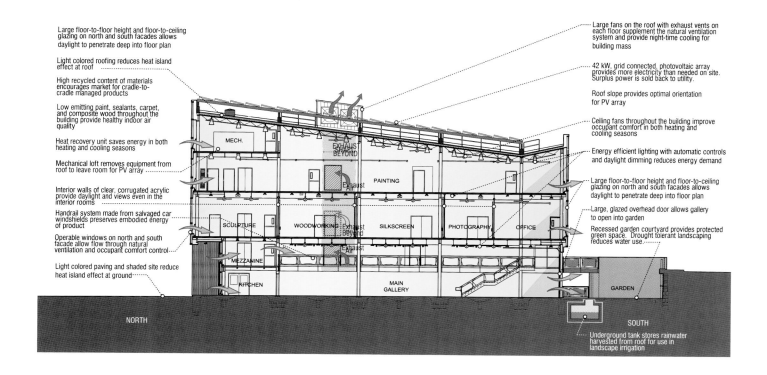

Large floor-to-floor height and floor-to-ceiling glazing on north and south facades allows daylight to penetrate deep into floor plan

Light colored roofing reduces heat island effect at roof

High recycled content of materials encourages market for cradle-to-cradle managed products

Low emitting paint, sealants, carpet, and composite wood throughout the building provide healthy indoor air quality

Heat recovery unit saves energy in both heating and cooling seasons

Mechanical loft removes equipment from roof to leave room for PV array

Interior walls of clear, corrugated acrylic provide daylight and views even in the interior rooms

Handrail system made from salvaged car windshields preserves embodied energy of product

Operable windows on north and south facade allow flow through natural ventilation and occupant comfort control

Light colored paving and shaded site reduce heat island effect at ground

Large fans on the roof with exhaust vents on each floor supplement the natural ventilation system and provide night-time cooling for building mass

42 kW, grid connected, photovoltaic array provides more electricity than needed on site. Surplus power is sold back to utility.

Roof slope provides optimal orientation for PV array

Ceiling fans throughout the building improve occupant comfort in both heating and cooling seasons

Energy efficient lighting with automatic controls and daylight dimming reduces energy demand

Large floor-to-floor height and floor-to-ceiling glazing on north and south facades allows daylight to penetrate deep into floor plan

Large, glazed overhead door allows gallery to open into garden

Recessed garden courtyard provides protected green space. Drought tolerant landscaping reduces water use.

Underground tank stores rainwater harvested from roof for use in landscape irrigation

MECH.

EXHAUST BEYOND

PAINTING

Exhaust

SCULPTURE

WOODWORKING

Exhaust Beyond

SILKSCREEN

PHOTOGRAPHY

OFFICE

Exhaust

MEZZANINE

KITCHEN

MAIN GALLERY

GARDEN

NORTH

SOUTH

TOP: Cladding and
photovoltaic array
MIDDLE: West elevation
BOTTOM: Gallery view

OPPOSITE
TOP LEFT: South elevation
TOP RIGHT: South elevation
BOTTOM: Gallery and
courtyard view

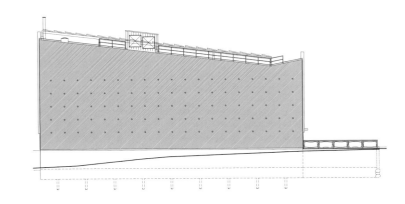

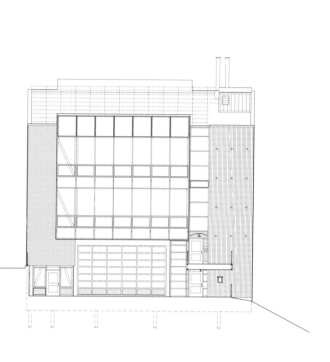

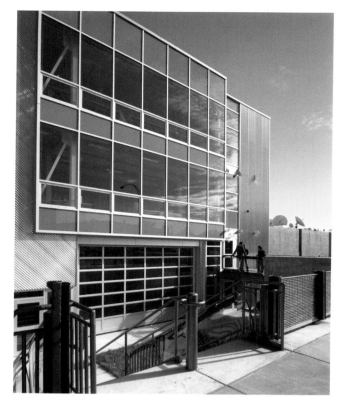

# Pittsburgh Glass Center

Pittsburgh, Pennsylvania

Davis Gardner Gannon Pope Architecture, Pittsburgh, Pennsylvania

**ARCHITECT:** Davis Gardner Gannon Pope Architecture, with Bruce Lindsey, Architect
**MECHANICAL ENGINEER:** Tudi Mechanical Systems
**PLUMBING ENGINEER:** Apex Plumbing
**LANDSCAPE ARCHITECT:** LaQuatra Bonci Associates
**CONSULTING ENGINEER:** Q-Dot: Michael Kokayko
**ENVIRONMENTAL BUILDING CONSULTANT:** Clearview Project Services Company
**ENVIRONMENTAL BUILDING CONSULTANT:** Sustainaissance International
This project is LEED-NC Gold certified.

The Pittsburgh Glass Center is an educational center for the glass arts. For their new 18,500-square-foot facility, the architects added a small circulation bar along the building's east side to the adaptive reuse of an existing masonry shell. Reuse is a dominant theme throughout the project and is central to its approach to integration. Material and energy inherent in the existing building are reused thoroughly in the project to minimize its total embodied energy and energy consumption. Like other projects, this is as much an economic impetus for a non-profit as it is an ecological impetus.

A key material that is salvaged from a different building is the corrugated glass facade. The material, its aluminum frames, and its hardware came from the renovation of a field house at Slippery Rock University, just north of Pittsburgh. In this case, the design of the de-installation of the salvaged material is as important as its installation in the new facility. This material clads the new circulation bar, providing an emblematic face to the building and pulling circulation out of the existing building and thereby maximizing its flexibility for adapting to future programs. Likewise, materials in this space, and throughout the building, use exposed fasteners and conduits that engender other types of adaptation as the needs and programs of the building change. This space contains radiant heating in the floor slab that modulates the operative temperature in the space against the heat loss of the glass envelope. Daylight in this and other spaces pervades the building. Eighty-two percent of the building is day lit with north-facing roof monitors, borrowed light from the corrugated glass-enclosed circulation bar, and direct side lighting.

The program—the production of glass works—is inherently energy intensive. Here heat produced in the production of glass is recovered and used to heat the building. A hydronic system exchanges heat from the hotshop kilns to smaller air handling units throughout the building. Air to air exhaust exchangers are also used in typical occupancies such as classrooms and offices. The offices use a simplified form of displacement ventilation located beneath work layout tables. The intense heat of the hotshops exaggerates the buoyancy of air in the building, providing excellent exhaust air flow. Supply side ventilation occurs through operable windows on the lower floor of the circulation bar and through the large glazed garage doors on the upper floor of the bar. To achieve this, the whole building is designed and classified as an atrium with connected hallways. This obviates the need for fire closures and dampers between adjacent spaces that would otherwise block the air and light patterns. Variances required this arrangement as a mixed-use code situation, as were additional fire sprinklers and fire-control systems.

Throughout this building, integrated design is characterized by an ambitious modesty that integrates the past, present, and future material functions of the building. The approach collapsed several material and energy systems into fewer physical, architectural systems. The mass of the existing building and the new construction are thermally active both as mechanical systems and as mass. The result is an intelligent, active, and durable sparseness that openly receives its program.

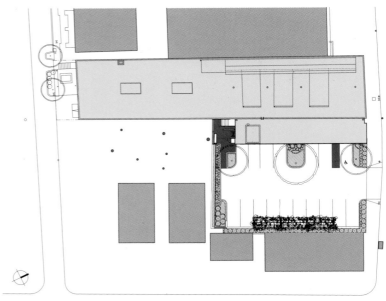

Site Plan

OPPOSITE
TOP: Renovated plans
BOTTOM: Building and courtyard/lot

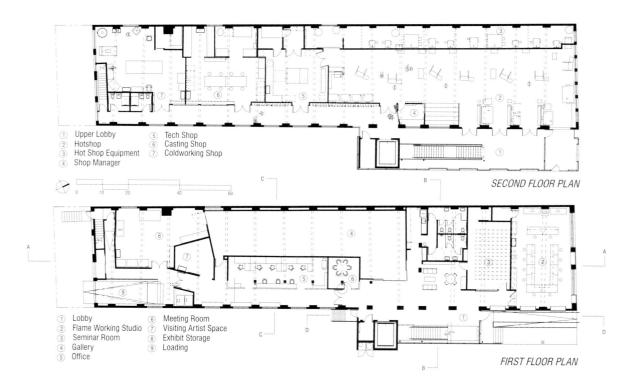

① Upper Lobby    ⑤ Tech Shop
② Hotshop    ⑥ Casting Shop
③ Hot Shop Equipment    ⑦ Coldworking Shop
④ Shop Manager

*SECOND FLOOR PLAN*

0    10    20    40    60

① Lobby    ⑥ Meeting Room
② Flame Working Studio    ⑦ Visiting Artist Space
③ Seminar Room    ⑧ Exhibit Storage
④ Gallery    ⑨ Loading
⑤ Office

*FIRST FLOOR PLAN*

TOP: Air, light, and people
circulation space
BOTTOM: Section at stair

OPPOSITE
TOP LEFT: New stair
TOP RIGHT: Street elevation
BOTTOM: Entry view

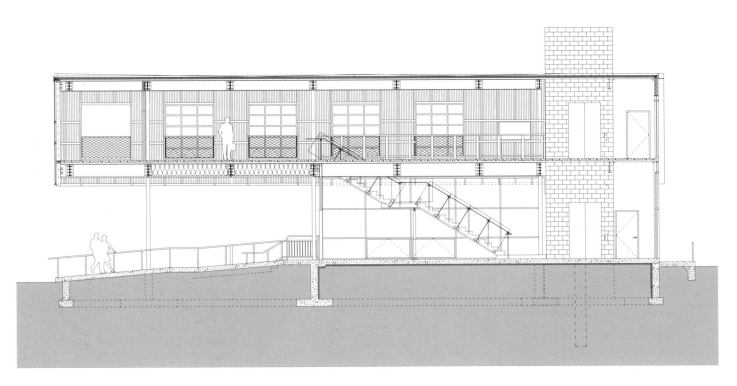

177

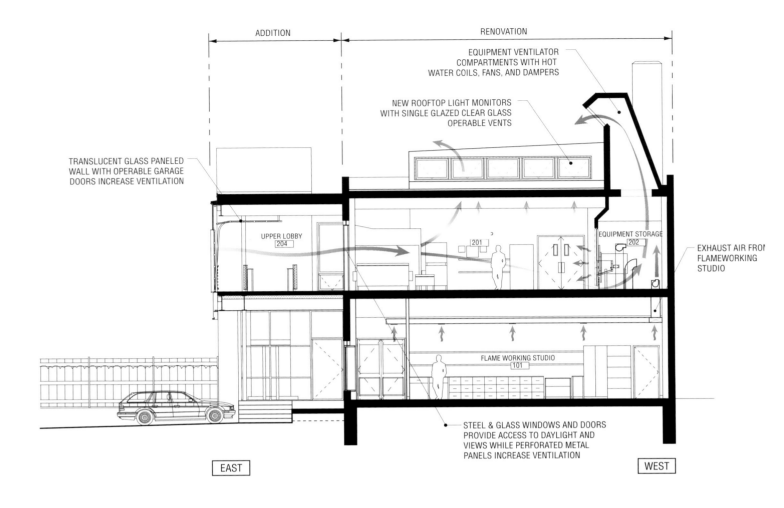

ADDITION | RENOVATION

EQUIPMENT VENTILATOR
COMPARTMENTS WITH HOT
WATER COILS, FANS, AND DAMPERS

NEW ROOFTOP LIGHT MONITORS
WITH SINGLE GLAZED CLEAR GLASS
OPERABLE VENTS

TRANSLUCENT GLASS PANELED
WALL WITH OPERABLE GARAGE
DOORS INCREASE VENTILATION

UPPER LOBBY
204

EQUIPMENT STORAGE
202

201

EXHAUST AIR FROM
FLAMEWORKING
STUDIO

FLAME WORKING STUDIO
101

STEEL & GLASS WINDOWS AND DOORS
PROVIDE ACCESS TO DAYLIGHT AND
VIEWS WHILE PERFORATED METAL
PANELS INCREASE VENTILATION

EAST | WEST

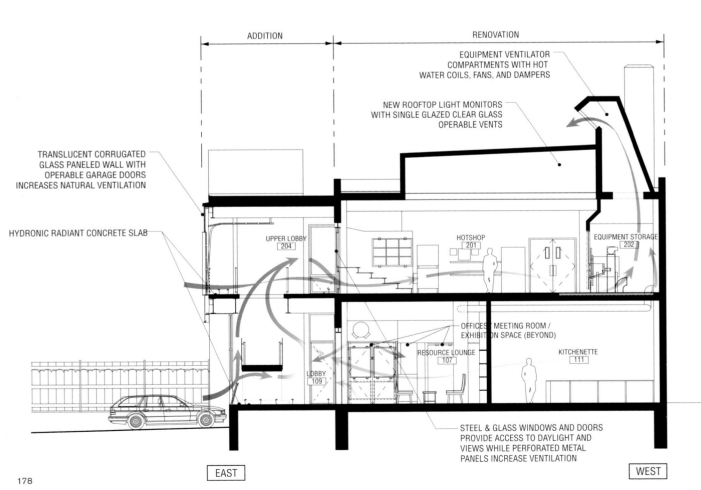

ADDITION | RENOVATION

EQUIPMENT VENTILATOR
COMPARTMENTS WITH HOT
WATER COILS, FANS, AND DAMPERS

NEW ROOFTOP LIGHT MONITORS
WITH SINGLE GLAZED CLEAR GLASS
OPERABLE VENTS

TRANSLUCENT CORRUGATED
GLASS PANELED WALL WITH
OPERABLE GARAGE DOORS
INCREASES NATURAL VENTILATION

HYDRONIC RADIANT CONCRETE SLAB

UPPER LOBBY
204

HOTSHOP
201

EQUIPMENT STORAGE
202

OFFICES / MEETING ROOM /
EXHIBITION SPACE (BEYOND)

RESOURCE LOUNGE
107

KITCHENETTE
111

LOBBY
109

STEEL & GLASS WINDOWS AND DOORS
PROVIDE ACCESS TO DAYLIGHT AND
VIEWS WHILE PERFORATED METAL
PANELS INCREASE VENTILATION

EAST | WEST

TOP LEFT: View of glass
studio
TOP RIGHT: Glass furnace
energy capture
BOTTOM: First floor air flow

OPPOSITE
Airflow diagrams

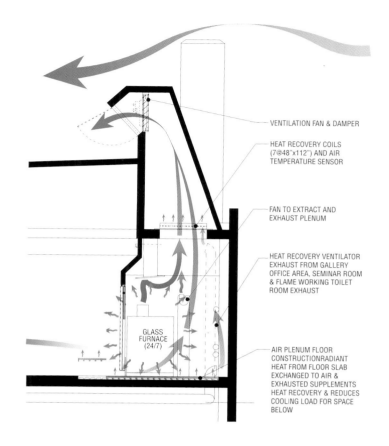

VENTILATION FAN & DAMPER

HEAT RECOVERY COILS
(7@48"x112") AND AIR
TEMPERATURE SENSOR

FAN TO EXTRACT AND
EXHAUST PLENUM

HEAT RECOVERY VENTILATOR
EXHAUST FROM GALLERY
OFFICE AREA, SEMINAR ROOM
& FLAME WORKING TOILET
ROOM EXHAUST

GLASS
FURNACE
(24/7)

AIR PLENUM FLOOR
CONSTRUCTIONRADIANT
HEAT FROM FLOOR SLAB
EXCHANGED TO AIR &
EXHAUSTED SUPPLEMENTS
HEAT RECOVERY & REDUCES
COOLING LOAD FOR SPACE
BELOW

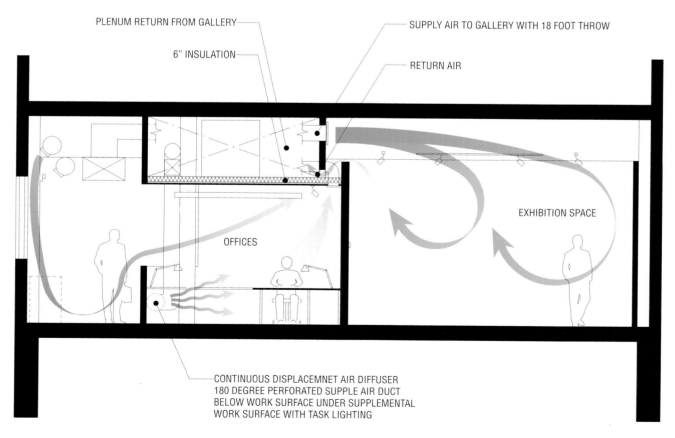

PLENUM RETURN FROM GALLERY

SUPPLY AIR TO GALLERY WITH 18 FOOT THROW

6" INSULATION

RETURN AIR

EXHIBITION SPACE

OFFICES

CONTINUOUS DISPLACEMNET AIR DIFFUSER
180 DEGREE PERFORATED SUPPLE AIR DUCT
BELOW WORK SURFACE UNDER SUPPLEMENTAL
WORK SURFACE WITH TASK LIGHTING

# Gleneagles Community Center

West Vancouver, British Columbia

Patkau Architects, Vancouver, British Columbia

ARCHITECT: Patkau Architects: John Patkau, Patricia Patkau, David Shone, Omer Arbel, Greg Boothroyd, Joanne Gates, Samantha Hayes, Patrick O'Sullivan, Craig Simms, Nick Sully
STRUCTURAL ENGINEER: Fast and Epp
MECHANICAL AND ELECTRICAL ENGINEER: Earth Tech Canada
LANDSCAPE ARCHITECT: Vaughan Landscape Planning and Design
CIVIL ENGINEER: Webster Engineering
SIGNAGE: Gallop/Varley
CODE CONSULTANT: Gage-Babcock and Associates
AUDIO VISUAL: Mc Squared System Design Group
CLIENT: District of West Vancouver
PHOTOGRAPHY: James Dow
PROJECT MANAGER: Maurice J. Ouellette Consulting
SPECIFICATIONS: Morris Specifications

The Gleneagles Community Center contains fitness, child care, art, gymnasium, and administrative facilities. The design integrates site, construction, and energy systems to help shape its architecture. The section of the building modified the cross-slope existing grade, creating two at-grade entrances at different levels on opposite sides of the building. The extended slope of the roof creates a deep, shaded porch that blocks heat gain and glare, which can be a problem in gymnasiums.

The concrete walls use tilt-up construction. The concrete used 26 percent fly ash in its mix. This reduced the carbon dioxide emissions for the concrete by 1,157 tons. These walls resolve the lateral structural forces of the building, but are also integral to the building's heating and cooling strategy. Cast into the walls are 6.8 kilometers of hydronic tubing. The floors and walls are thus thermally active surfaces, as well as structural. These surfaces serve as the building's heating and cooling system. This system is based upon the Swiss BATISO system, a heating and cooling strategy based upon control of surface temperatures rather than air temperatures. The minimal amount of forced air is designed only for fresh air displacement ventilation with no heating or cooling requirements. In this configuration, the mean radiant temperature of the thermal masses is the controlling system that provides a comfortable operable temperature. The primary energy source for this building is a heat pump supplied by a shallow ground loop geothermal system embedded in the adjacent parking lot.

The building section channels and captures buoyant air at its peak. Air heat exchangers capture the heat from the exhaust air to preheat the low-velocity displacement ventilation air when necessary. The project also includes a small heat exchanger in a meeting room on the southeast corner of the building that captures morning sun and warms this small room. Since the architecture surfaces are the primary heating and cooling device and thus not dependent upon air volume temperature, doors and windows can be open at any time without compromising the system's performance.

Roof stormwater drainage is captured and channeled by a trough at the lower edge of the roof that catches water from the gutter above. The parking lot uses pervious paving and grading that directs water to a bioswale. Both of these systems feed into a sequence of constructed wetlands in the adjacent golf course that slow and filter site stormwater before entering the adjacent and important salmon habitat watershed. One hundred percent of the stormwater is managed on site.

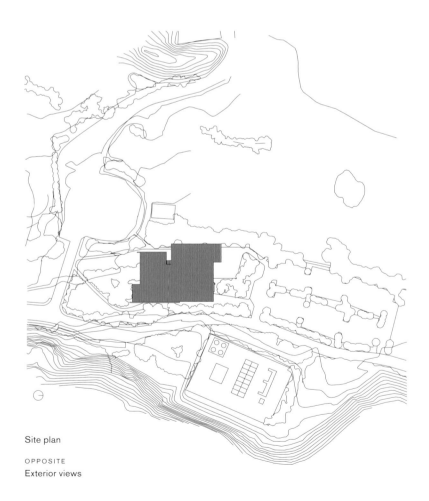

Site plan

OPPOSITE
Exterior views

The building section also modulates light patterns. The large roof and overhang blocks direct light from the gymnasium, allowing a generous glazed wall on its edge for diffused daylight and visual connections to the outside. All primary programmed spaces enjoy access to daylight, saving superfluous electrical loads and heat gain. The integrated strategies pursued in this building make sense from energy and construction standpoints but they are primarily deployed in service of an open and durable community program.

0       20 ft

15

8      4 8
       13     12
              8      11

Upper Level

**Upper Floor**
11 Fitness
12 Reception
13 Training Studio
14 Counseling
15 Open to Below

15          15

9

8
8   7   6   2   3 4   5

10

1       1

Main Floor

**Main floor**
1 Entry Porch
2 "Living Room"
3 Cafe
4 Meeting Room
5 Fire Place Lounge
6 Reception
7 Administration
8 Office
9 Childcare
10 Children's Playground
15 Open to Below

26          24          21
                              16

25

22
20   23   25   20   19       18
          19              17

Lower Floor

**Lower Floor**
16 Workshop
17 Art Studio
18 Maintenance
19 Mechanical
20 Electrical
21 Workshop Courtyard
22 Kitchen
23 Youth Lounge
24 Gymnasium
25 Storage
26 Multipurpose

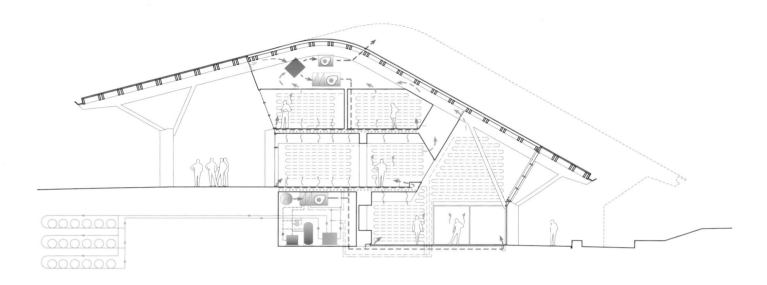

# Water + Life Museums

## Hemet, California

---

## Lehrer + Gangi Design + Build, Los Angeles, California

**ARCHITECTS:** Lehrer + Gangi Design + Build
Michael B. Lehrer, Principal; Mark Gangi, Co-Lead Design
Principal; Frank P. Gangi, Construction Manager; Anne
Marie Kaufman Perlov, Project Architect; Project Team:
Jonathan Dawang, Steve Deyer, Jovan Gayton, Monica
Grau, Han Hsieh, Nerin Kadribegovic, Chris Mundweil,
Yuri Osipov, Maria Rockstroh, Robin Sakahara
**MECHANICAL ENGINEER:** IBE Consulting Engineers
**STRUCTURAL ENGINEER:** Nabih Youssef & Associates
**LANDSCAPE ARCHITECT:** mia lehrer + associates
**CIVIL ENGINEER:** KPFF Consulting Engineers
**ELECTRICAL AND SOLAR ENGINEER:** Vector Delta
Design Group
**LEED PROGRAM MANAGEMENT:** Zinner Consulting
This project anticipates LEED Platinum certification.

The Diamond Valley Lake Reservoir is a Metropolitan
Water District of Southern California project for creating
an emergency fresh water reservoir. During the reservoir's
significant amount of excavation and earth moving, several
fossils were discovered. The 62,000-square-foot Water
+ Life Lakes Museum complex consists of two museums,
classrooms, laboratories, auditoriums, and a landscape
campus that houses these artifacts and educates the public
about the project and the role of water. The Western Center
for Archeology and Paleontology contains the fossils and
artifacts unearthed in the construction of the reservoir.
The other museum, The Center for Water Education,
focuses on education and water stewardship. The design
of the building and the adjacent landscape aligns with the
resource conservation and knowledge-based mission of the
program.

One of the largest institutional photovoltaic arrays in
the world serves the building. A 3000-panel, 540-kilowatt
photovoltaic array yields two-thirds of the building's energy
demand, placing it beyond California's Title 24 energy
code. The array is nearly flat and shades the roof membrane
below. The building utilizes radiant heating and cooling to
condition the operative temperature of the interior. As with
any building, a key aspect of this building's energy strategy
is the minimization of heat gains. The eastern and western
glazed exposures are each shaded by solar control devices
of steel slats and printed plastic banners. The flat roof
uses the photovoltaic array to shade a low albedo white
membrane, minimizing the heat island effect, building fabric
heat gains, and extending the life of the roof membrane.
Occupancy sensors and daylight sensors work in tandem to
optimize light conditions, only demanding electricity when
needed.

The building and landscape overtly work to collect
stormwater and direct it to the water table. A drip system
uses some of this water to irrigate the campus's drought
tolerant landscape, developed by Mia Lehrer + Associates.
The landscape also makes use of many sculptural stones
from the excavation and construction of the Diamond Valley
Lake dam. The landscape extends the museum educational
functions into the landscape.

The project was completed as a partnership between
Michael Lehrer and Mark Gangi. This design-build
partnership, along with their team of consultants, was
fundamental to the integrated design of this project.

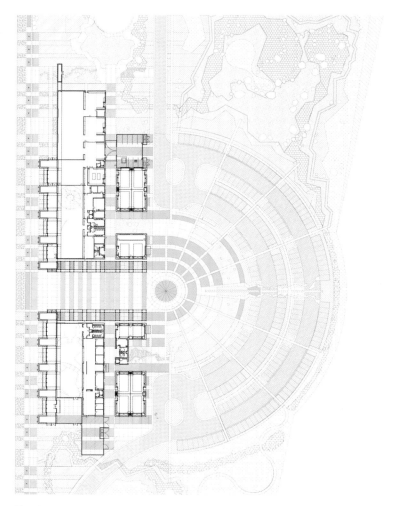

Site plan

OPPOSITE
Arrival court

Systems diagram

OPPOSITE
TOP: Sun screen structure
BOTTOM: PV solar control

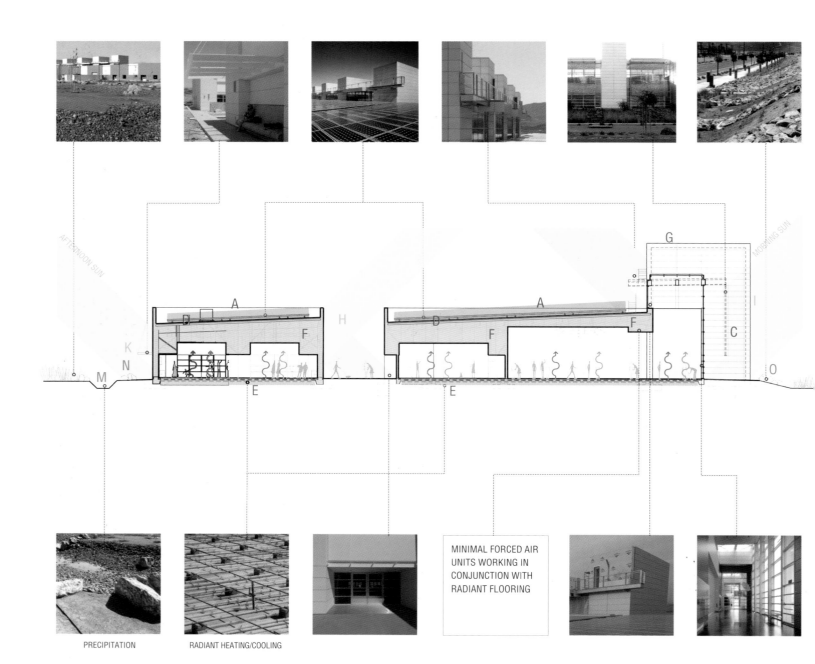

PRECIPITATION

RADIANT HEATING/COOLING

MINIMAL FORCED AIR
UNITS WORKING IN
CONJUNCTION WITH
RADIANT FLOORING

Ⓗ REFLECTED SUN LIGHT
REFLECTED SUN LIGHT PROVIDES AMBIENT
NATURAL LIGHT IN OFFICES WHILE OVER-
HANGS REDUCE SOLAR HEAT GAIN.

Ⓘ DAYLIGHT
HIGH-PERFORMANCE GLASS CURTAIN WALL
CONTRIBUTES TO 75% OF BUILDING BEING
DAYLIT.

Ⓚ AWNINGS
AWNINGS ON WEST FACADE PROTECT
FROM AFTERNOON SUN.

Ⓛ SUN SHADING
ROOF OVERHANG AND CATWALK PROVIDE
SUN SHADING FOR WESTERN CLERESTORY.

Ⓜ LANDSCAPE
ABSTRACT XERISCAPE OF NATIVE ROCKS,
PLANTS, AND GRASSES REDUCES NEED
FOR IRRIGATION.

Ⓝ LANDSCAPE
NATIVE ROCKS AND GRASSES ARE SUS-
TAINED BY A STATE-OF-THE-ART DRIP
IRRIGATION SYSTEM.

Ⓞ PRECIPITATION MANAGEMENT
ON SITE PRECIPITATION MANAGEMENT
VIA ROCKY SWALES RECREATE NATURE'S
BRAIDED STREAMS.

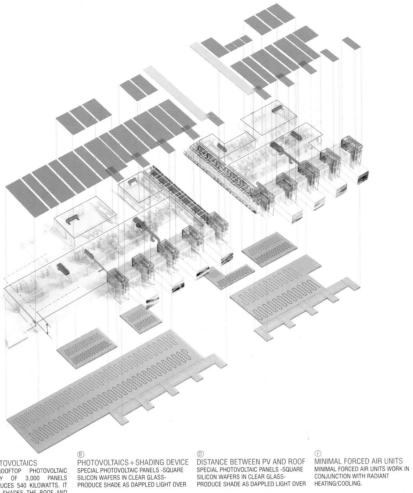

Ⓐ
**PHOTOVOLTAICS**
A ROOFTOP PHOTOVOLTAIC ARRAY OF 3,000 PANELS PRODUCES 540 KILOWATTS. IT ALSO SHADES THE ROOF AND WILL PROLONG THE LIFE OF THE ROOF COVERING BY ABOUT 25%. THE SYSTEM WILL PROVIDE A PROJECTED SAVINGS OVER BUILDINGS LIFESPAN OF ABOUT $13 MILLION.

Ⓑ
**PHOTOVOLTAICS + SHADING DEVICE**
SPECIAL PHOTOVOLTAIC PANELS -SQUARE SILICON WAFERS IN CLEAR GLASS- PRODUCE SHADE AS DAPPLED LIGHT OVER

Ⓒ
**SHADING DEVICE**
TRANSLUCENT BANNERS SHADE THE EAST FACADE TO MITIGATE HEAT RADIATION.

Ⓓ
**DISTANCE BETWEEN PV AND ROOF**
SPECIAL PHOTOVOLTAIC PANELS -SQUARE SILICON WAFERS IN CLEAR GLASS- PRODUCE SHADE AS DAPPLED LIGHT OVER

Ⓔ
**RADIANT HEATING + COOLING**
A RADIANT HEATING AND COOLING FLOOR SYSTEM IS FOUND THROUGHOUT THE BUILDING.

Ⓕ
**MINIMAL FORCED AIR UNITS**
MINIMAL FORCED AIR UNITS WORK IN CONJUNCTION WITH RADIANT HEATING/COOLING.

Ⓖ
**INSULATION**
THICK WALL INSULATION MITIGATES COOLING LOSS TO EXTERIOR.

# U.S. Border Patrol Station

Murrieta, California

———

Garrison Architects, Brooklyn, New York

ARCHITECTS: Garrison Architects: Ryan Cole, James Garrison, Mark Gordon, Kristan Gregerson Herbing, Samantha Whitney
ENGINEER: Arup
LANDSCAPE ARCHITECT: Mia Lehrer and Associates
CIVIL ENGINEER: Flores Lund Consultants
LIGHTING DESIGN: Cline Bettridge Bernstein Lighting Design
CONSTRUCTION MANAGER: Analytical Planning Systems
CLIENT: U.S. General Services Administration, Steve Baker

The 40,000-square-foot U.S. Border Patrol Station integrates several aspects of its context. The project overtly responds to the social and cultural landscape of the border while also engaging the physical landscape and climate of its region. The project is located in the dry and hot Temecula Valley in southern California. The building houses facilities for the border patrol agent squads and administration as well as detention areas.

The intense sun in this climate is a primary concern for the building. The building is organized along a north-south axis. This configuration allows diffuse daylight to punctuate the space, but with little direct heat gain. The eastern, entry facade is a tilted Cor-Ten steel wall that alludes to the steel walls used along the border and emblematically restates the contentious social situation of the program. On the west side of the building, the ground mounds up around the building, blocking the intensity of the low western sun. The south side of the building features deep solar-control devices that shade the windows and walls on this exposure, which opens up as the building's public entrance. The building palette—corrugated metal, shaded concrete masonry units, and glazing—continues into the building's interior. The hues of the palette all relate to the hues of the adjacent landscape.

The building captures and channels the available light, wind, and water on its site. The surface of the skylights and clerestory transoms are patterned similarly to a Fresnel lens, diffusing the light and avoiding the glare of the strong solar energy. Full height glass walls only occur at the narrow north and south ends of the primary corridor. The daylight works to illuminate, save energy, and acclimatize throughout the building interior. The thermal mass of the building's concrete and concrete masonry-unit walls modulate the temperature swings of the arid region. The wind on the site is drawn in low on the west side of the building and exhausted high through operable louvers on the east

exposure for good air quality. This ventilation strategy also helps modulate the temperature of the space.

The building also captures and channels its stormwater into the arid adjacent landscape. A series of gravel swales, with drought-tolerant local plants, capture the water and extend the logic of the building's composition into the landscape. The logic of the landscape, however, also inversely guides the building's section. A landscaped berm on the western exposed side blocks low afternoon and evening sun, and the building massing recedes into the rolling topography of the adjacent landscape.

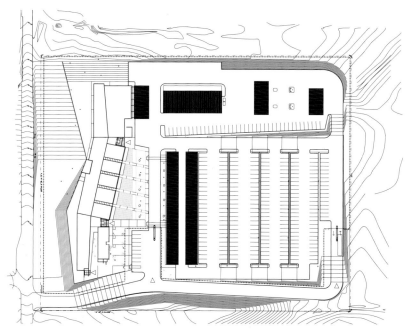

Site plan

OPPOSITE
TOP: Cor-Ten wall
BOTTOM: Deep southern solar control at entry

TOP: Interior view with daylight monitor
BOTTOM: Building section

OPPOSITE
TOP LEFT: Daylight diffusion
LEFT: Solar path plan diagram
TOP RIGHT: Corridor view
BOTTOM: Plan

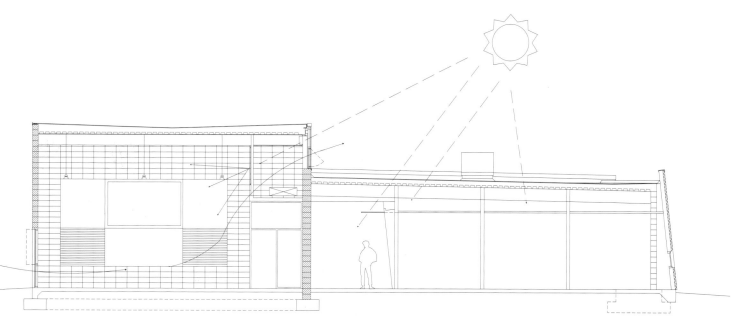

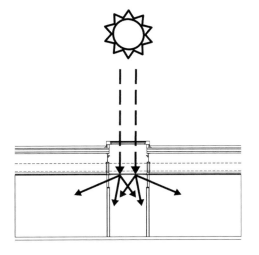

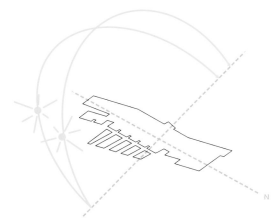

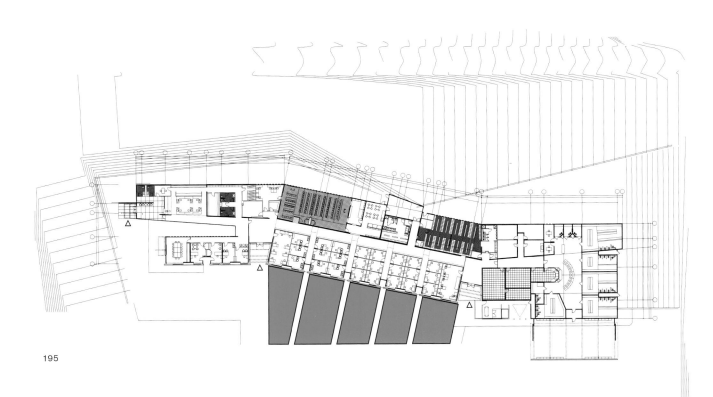

# Fire Station 10

Seattle, Washington

---

Weinstein A|U Architects and Urban Designers, Seattle, Washington

**ARCHITECT:** Weinstein A|U Architects and Urban Designers: Ed Weinstein, Principal, Milton Won, Project Manager; Jon A Mihkels, Project Architect
**ASSOCIATE ARCHITECT:** RossDrulisCusenbery Architecture
**CIVIL AND STRUCTURAL ENGINEER:** Magnusson Klemencic Associates
**MECHANICAL ENGINEER:** Notkin Engineering
**LANDSCAPE ARCHITECT:** Gustafson Guthrie Nichol
**LIGHTING CONSULTANT:** Candela
**INDEPENDENT COST ESTIMATING:** Davis Langdon
**ACOUSTICAL CONSULTANT:** SSA Acoustics
**GENERAL CONTRACTOR AND CONSTRUCTION MANAGEMENT:** Hoffman Construction Company
**CLIENT:** City of Seattle
**ELECTRICAL & TECHNOLOGY:** Sparling
**AUDIO VISUAL:** Alta Consulting Services
**FIRE STATION CONSULTING ARCHITECT:** TCA
**SUSTAINABILITY CONSULTANT:** Paladino and Company
**GREEN ROOF CONSULTANT:** Roofscapes
**SPECIFICATIONS CONSULTANT:** Eskilsson Architecture

The new Fire Station 10 replaces a vintage fire station and consolidates Seattle's 15,000-square-foot Emergency Operations Center (EOC) and 15,000-square-foot Fire Alarm Center (FAC) and 911 Fire and Medical Dispatch Center. All together, the 61,000 square feet occupy a steeply sloped site with a fifty-eight-foot grade change and an elevated roadway to the north. This essential facility must be able to operate independently for at least seventy-two hours during a disaster.

The integration of a sloping site with the requirements of the complex program provided the impetus for the building's organization. The flat, six-bay drive-through fire apparatus portion of the program connects points of similar elevation on the cross slope. The fire station residences are above the long-span equipment bay. The other program areas straddle the apparatus bay on the high and low sides of the site. The Fire Alarm Center and 911 Dispatch facility sits atop the Emergency Operations Center on the upper portion of the site. The fire station administration program occupies the lower portion of the site. The upper portions of the facility are articulated as a metal volume sitting on a masonry plinth below.

The City of Seattle requires all new municipal facilities to meet a level of energy performance, human comfort, and health. These requirements fundamentally align with the requirements of the program and its need for independent operation during a disaster. Minimizing water and energy operation requirements is essential to the operation of the facility during a disaster. The energy performance measures in this building include demand control ventilation; high-

efficiency lighting, air handling and filtration units, and glazing units; and highly insulated building envelopes. Solar-control devices help articulate and shade glazed apertures. Skylights top the 911 call center. The daylight strategies and improved indoor air quality also align with the program; these strategies help amend the inherently stressful work environment for employees in the 911 call centers and Emergency Operations Center.

The firefighters require periodic equipment tests and drills. Previously, these hose tests were conducted off-site. In the new facility, the team will use an on-site fire hydrant and spray the rear wall of the apron where a trench drain will collect the water in a cistern that also collects water from the roof. The cistern supplies all the water required for the landscaping on-site and for washing the fire trucks. Regular stormwater is also mitigated by the new facility. The topographic modifications, 20 percent landscaped site area, and a 15,000-square-foot extensive, vegetated roof together dampen and reduce stormwater events.

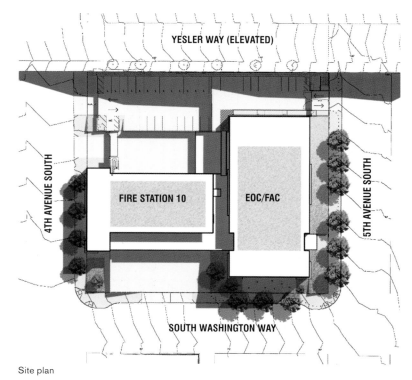

Site plan

OPPOSITE
TOP: Southeast view of the EOC and FAC
BOTTOM: Southwest view of fire station

In the case of Fire Station 10, programmatic and code requirements provide the impetus for an integrated design. However, and more importantly, the integrated design solutions serve to amplify and the practices of the building occupants while minimizing their impact on resources.

TOP: Water collection and reuse strategy
BOTTOM: Solar-control studies

OPPOSITE
TOP: Program organization
BOTTOM: South elevation, South Washington Street

1. 12,000 Gallon Cistern
2. Sediment Filter
3. Pump Vault
4. Hose Drill Wall with Water Collection Trough
5. Site Stormwater Detention, 36,000 Gallons
6. Stormwater Monitoring Station for Vegetated and Non-vegetated Roofs
7. Vegetated Roof, 16,000 Square Feet
8. Non-vegetated Ballasted Roof
9. Landscaped Areas
10. Cistern Overflow
11. Fire Hydrant (for Hose Drilling)
12. Truck Washing

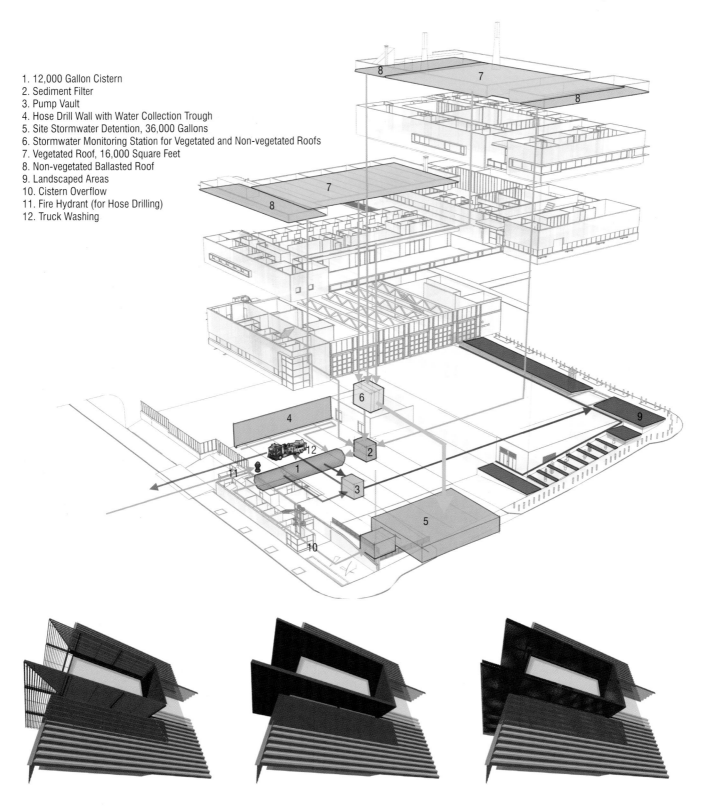

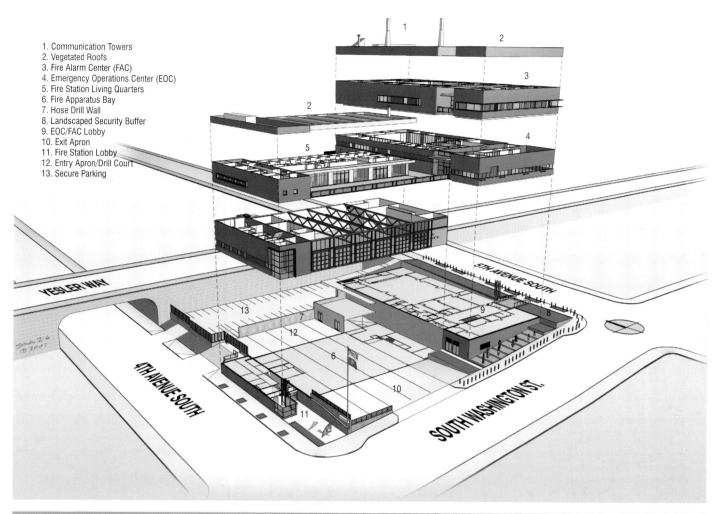

1. Communication Towers
2. Vegetated Roofs
3. Fire Alarm Center (FAC)
4. Emergency Operations Center (EOC)
5. Fire Station Living Quarters
6. Fire Apparatus Bay
7. Hose Drill Wall
8. Landscaped Security Buffer
9. EOC/FAC Lobby
10. Exit Apron
11. Fire Station Lobby
12. Entry Apron/Drill Court
13. Secure Parking

YESLER WAY

4TH AVENUE SOUTH

5TH AVENUE SOUTH

SOUTH WASHINGTON ST.

TOP: East-west section
perspective
BOTTOM: Construction

OPPOSITE
TOP: North-south section
perspective
BOTTOM: Construction

1. Apparatus Bays
2. Support
3. Classroom
4. Living Quarters
5. Vegetated Roof
6. Mechanical/Electrical
7. EOC Operations Room
8. Break-out Conference Room
9. FAC 911 Dispatch
10. Living Quarters
11. Sleep Quarters
12. Skylights

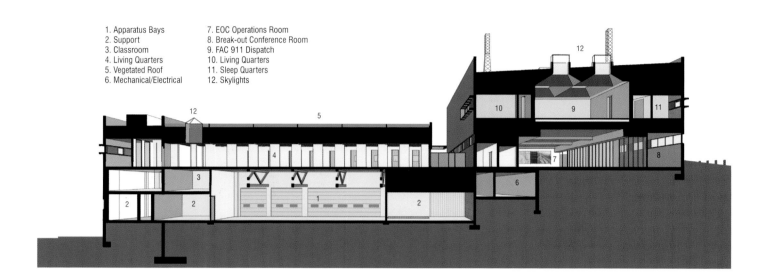

1. Apparatus Bays
2. Sleeping Quarters
3. Restrooms/Showers
4. Beanery/Exercise
5. Terrace
6. Back Apron
7. Front Apron
8. Water Cistern
9. Water Detention
10. Parking/Future Fire Administration Headquarters
11. Vegetated Roof
12. Drill Wall

# Acknowledgments

I would like to thank, foremost, the integrated practices of architects, engineers, consultants, and their administrative staffs who supported this book through their contributions of drawings, diagrams, background material, and their enthusiasm for the project; the photographers who agreed to include their work; my superb colleagues at the Northeastern University School of Architecture; and to editors Jennifer Thompson and Lauren Nelson Packard for making hard work seem so easy.

# Photography Credits

U.S. Federal Building
All photos © Tim Griffith/ESTO

The Bank of America Tower at One Bryant Park
p. 25, 26 bottom, 29 © dbox
p. 27 bottom © Screampoint

Lovejoy Building
All photos © Gene Faulkner

290 Mulberry
All photos © SHoP Architects

557/559
All photos © Robert Knight

DDBC Model Residence One
All photos © Liam Frederick

ecoMOD
All photos © Scott Smith

Chicago Residence
p. 73, 75 top & bottom, p. 77 top left and right, p. 77 bottom
right, p. 78, p. 80 top © Jon Miller/Hedrich Blessing

p. 76 top, p. 77 bottom right, © Steve Hall/Hedrich
Blessing

p. 77 bottom left, p. 79 all, p. 80 bottom, p. 81 top left and
right © Wheeler Kearns Architects

New Residence at the Swiss Embassy
p. 83 top and bottom, p. 88 bottom left, p. 87 bottom right
© Andy Ryan P. 84, p. 85 © Prakash Pratel

Museum of Contemporary Art, Denver
p. 95 top: © Adjaye Associates
p. 95 bottom left and right © Carsten Boschen

North Carolina Museum of Art
Renderings by dbox: p. 97 top and bottom, p. 98 bottom, p.
99 top and bottom,  p. 100 top and bottom, p. 101 top and
bottom. Renderings by Vigilism: p. 96, p. 98 top,
Other Renderings by Thomas Phifer and Partners

The Glass Pavilion at the Toledo Art Museum
All photos © SANAA
P. 106, 107 Structural Analysis Models courtesy Guy
Nordenson and Associates Structural Engineers LLP
P. 108 CFD Analysis Models courtesy Transsolar
P. 109 Day Lighting Analysis Models courtesy Arup Lighting

Crown Hall Restoration
p. .113 top and bottom © Ron Gordon
p. 114, 115 © Krueck and Sexton Architects

Lavin-Bernick Center for University Life
All photos © Paul Crosby

Seminar II Building at the Evergreen State College
p. 128: © Aerolistphoto.com
p. 129, 130 bottom, 132 bottom: © Lara Swimmer/ESTO
p. 131 top left, 133 top left, 133 top right, 133 bottom right:
© Katie Wellman
p. 131 top right, 133 bottom left: © Mahlum Architects
p. 132 top: © Murase Associates

Interdisciplinary Science & Technology Building 2
All photos © Bill Timmerman

University of Arizona College of Architecture and
Landscape Architecture
All photos © Michael Shanks

Sidwell Friends School Middle School Renovation and
Addition
p. 155, p. 158 bottom, p. 160 bottom, p. 159 bottom,: ©
Barry Halkin
p. 156 top, p. 157 bottom, p. 159 bottom: ©  Peter Aaron/
ESTO

Artists for Humanity EpiCenter
p. 169 top © Peter Vanderwarker
p. 169 bottom, p. 171 bottom, p. 172 top left, p. 172 bottom,
p. 173 top right, p. 174 bottom: © Richard Mandelkorn

Pittsburgh Glass Center
All photos © Ed Massery

Gleneagles Community Center
All photos © James Dow

Water + Life Museums
p. 187, p. 189 all, p. 190 bottom: © Fotoworks
p. 189 all: © Lehrer Gangi

U.S. Border Patrol Station
All photos © Fotoworks

Fire Station 10
All photos © Michael Burns

All drawings and diagrams contributed by each architect
and their consultants.